Explorations in Indian Philosophy

Explorations in Indian Philosophy

Rajendran Chettiarthodi

With a Foreword by
Mrinal Kaul

DK PRINTWORLD
Publishers of Indian Traditions

Cataloging in Publication Data — DK
[Courtesy: D.K. Agencies (P) Ltd. <docinfo@dkagencies.com>]

Rajendran, C. (Chettiarthodi), 1952- **author.**
Explorations in Indian philosophy / Rajendran Chettiarthodi ; with a foreword by Mrinal Kaul.
pages cm
Includes passages in Sanskrit (roman).
Includes bibliographical references and index.
ISBN 9788124610350 (Hb)

1. Philosophy, Indic. 2. Hindu philosophy. I. Title.

LCC B131.R35 2020 | DDC 181.4 23

ISBN: 978-81-246-1035-0 (Hb)

First published in India in 2020

Printed and published by:
D.K. Printworld (P) Ltd.
Regd. Office : "Vedaśrī", F-395, Sudarshan Park
ESI Hospital Metro Station, New Delhi - 110015
Phones : (011) 2545 3975, 2546 6019
e-mail : indology@dkprintworld.com
Web : www.dkprintworld.com

Foreword

*Mrinal Kaul**

DURING my recent research visit to Bhandarkar Oriental Research Institute in Pune I met a bright young Sanskrit student who had just submitted his doctoral thesis on Advaita Vedānta. After a couple of discussions he was really keen to show me his thesis. The thesis was a newly edited Sanskrit text along with translation and annotations and some philosophical discussion about the content of the text. It was a good work, however I was not too happy to see a two-page bibliography in an almost three-hundred page thesis. When I asked the student why he had not considered reading or referring to some crucial secondary sources, for instance, what Bina Gupta or Chakravarthi Ram-Prasad ventured into or what Stephen H. Phillips or Jonardon Ganeri were "doing" or what a certain Michael Comans or Sthaneshwar Timalsina thought about the problematics of the Advaita Vedānta, he showed complete disdain saying he was not interested in their works. In a somewhat shy, but audacious tone he said he was interested in the Sanskrit text alone. Incidentally, a certain other student who also sounded well trained in Sanskrit pedagogy and was wanting to pursue his doctoral research in Indian philosophy also called me a couple of weeks before I was in Pune. In a relatively longer conversation when I asked him – "have you read Daya Krishna?", he replied that he was not interested in "that kind of stuff" with a

* Assistant Professor, Manipal Centre for Humanities, Manipal Academy of Higher Education (MAHE), Manipal, mrinal.kaul@stx.oxon.org

somewhat derogatory tone. I immediately got transported to my own student days in a department of Sanskrit in a university in India where we were trained to feel proud being the custodians of a heritage that one was supposed to protect, preserve and preach, but never apply "contradictory thinking" to it. It was only after half a decade that, when I discovered the writings of Daya Krishna and other thinkers like him on my own, I began to ask myself why was I not made aware of his writings when I was specializing in "Indian philosophy" in a department of Sanskrit. I thought it was an injustice done to me by my teachers. I should also have been introduced to fresh critical writings on Indian philosophy irrespective of the fact whether my teachers or I agreed or disagreed with Daya Krishna's viewpoints. But my shock intensified recently when I discovered that even my teachers who taught me Indian philosophy are still unaware of the writings of Daya Krishna and K.C. Bhattacharyya. I have been wondering why should that be the case! I have heard a large number of philosophers (who are not interested in philology) accusing philologists and I have also witnessed ample number of philologists (who may also be interested in philosophy) blaming philosophers (who may also be interested in philology). Each time I have been appalled with a certain bizarre audacity with which either of these camps might dismiss each other. Unfortunately, over a period of time this is what has created an alarming gulf between the two methodological approaches that are otherwise supposed to go hand-in-hand. This should allow me to elaborate upon what I have wanted to say. (For more on such questions see Raghuramaraju 2006: 13ff and also Coquereau-Saouma 2018 in Coquereau-Saouma et al. 2018).

In this Foreword I have purposely meant to be critical of the author of this book by attempting to displace the fossilized discourse on "Indian philosophy" and at the same time greatly appreciating his insights within that set discourse. On the one hand I strongly believe that the discourse on Indian philosophy is to be completely taken outside the box within which we have confined it for a longer period of time, breaking the age-old chains of obsolete methods used for evaluating thinking patterns, on the other hand, I am firm on the opinion that the Indian philosophical discourse studied only through Sanskrit sources also has to be displaced. This has to be done by asking uncomfortable and provocative questions that someone like Daya Krishna was not tired of asking. And this has also to be done, at the same time, by not neglecting the uncomfortable and provocative questions that traditional Sanskrit *paṇḍits* are asking, even if done only through oral discourses; their questions often do not catch our attention only because they are very often not recorded.

One might pose a certain valid question – why one more book on "Indian philosophy" when there are already so many others available to us. Indeed there has been no dearth of sound scholarship on "Indian philosophy" particularly in the past couple of decades. Certainly it is because of the assiduous efforts of many of my learned colleagues that the classical and contemporary discourses on philosophy in South Asia is gradually finding a global platform. In fact, the state of affairs of Indian philosophy in the higher education system of India itself seems to be rather dismal. Nonetheless, there is hope lingering at many levels. One hope is certainly a book like this that is written by an eminent scholar asking many questions and complicating many ideas closely rather than only either attempting to write another history or another introductory book on "Indian philosophy". Having said that we have also witnessed some very important introductory books on "Indian philosophy" in the recent past those have made every effort to bring critical insights, neither just introducing them nor repeating the old narratives about proven facts (see Gupta 2012; King 1999a; Perrett 2016 to mention only a few). But this is not as easy as it may sound. In fact, it is much more challenging in the case of South Asia. Let me explain.

First of all the term "Indian" itself is very complex and complicated, and thus it needs to be problematized. Here I am referring to the term "Indian" breaking it down, as a Naiyāyika would do, to the abstract notion of "Indian-ness". As A.K. Ramanujan (1999: 34ff) questioned – what is this "Indian-ness" and how do we make sense of it and thus engage with whatever it may mean? This is important for me as I write this Foreword for a book on "Indian philosophy" I do need to draw attention of the readers towards what one may mean by "Indian-ness" of philosophy. How does philosophy or any academic discipline become Indian or American or Japanese, etc.? Or how does a particular way of thinking become Indian or Iranian or Pakistani? Or, to take another example, how is Indian Buddhism different from Tibetan Buddhism, or different from American Buddhism, or from Thai Buddhism, or from the ancient "Afghani" Buddhism that was being practised in what is today's Afghanistan. Or how is purely political Buddhism of B.R. Ambedkar in the twentieth century CE different from all these Buddhisms? Is "Indian-ness" merely the geographical territory or the nation state idea? We, in fact, know and understand why Allama Iqbal "is" not an "Indian philosopher", at least not in the Indian discourse within India. Thought patterns embedded in thinking consciousness are no slave of the ideologies of a certain nation state, be it ancient or modern. Yes, of course, the geopolitical situation of a certain nation state may give rise to a specific political philosophy in a particular region. Thus the political and social philosophy as it develops over a period of time in Kashmir may have altogether different concerns than the concerns it may develop, for instance, in Kerala or Bengal. But the "Indian" in my passport is not the same as the "Indian" in "Indian philosophy" even though both are referring to the same territory.

I may be allowed to make absurd assertions to complicate it further: Is someone like Gayatri Chakravorty Spivak an Indian or a Bengali or an American or a subaltern theorist/scholar/ philosopher? An ethnic Bengali, holding Indian nationality, teaching in an American university theorizing subaltern – is her philosophy Indian just because she is an Indian national or is her theoretical approach Indian just because she is making use of a number of Bengali works or does it become simply American since she is teaching in an institution that is located in a country called America? Her theoretical approach can neither be called Indian, nor American. At a certain abstract theoretical level, I do agree that the binaries of East and West do cease to exist. In that case if someone might ask – does that mean someone like Śaṅkara was not an "Indian" philosopher? Of course, he was, but the point I am making is that one needs to understand what was "Indian" about him as a "philosopher". It cannot be simply reduced down to the fact that he was an Indian philosopher just because he was born in ancient India or because he was writing in Sanskrit or he was reviving Vedānta even though all of these elements would form a part of his "Indian-ness" as well. Or one should even ask what was the idea of "India" in Śaṅkara's time. Or was Śaṅkara even bothered about whatever the idea of "India" or "Indian-ness" would have been? And if we go by the nation state idea, then the ancient Sanskrit grammarian Pāṇini was an Afghani or a Pakistani considering he belonged to Śalāturīya that historians have located somewhere between today's Afghanistan (ancient Gandhāra) and Pakistan. So as Bina Gupta would maintain, we are not talking about a geographical territory or a nation state idea when we talk about "Indian" in the context of "Indian philosophy":

> It is indeed anachronistic to give a geographical adjective to a mode of thinking, unless one agrees with Nietzsche's statement that Indian philosophy has something to do with the Indian food and climate, and German Idealism with the German love of beer. There must be some way of characterizing a philosophical tradition other than identifying such contingent features as the geographical and historical milieu in which it was born, some way of identifying it by its concepts and logic, the problems, the methods, and other issues that are internal to the tradition under consideration. – Gupta 2012: 3

So what is the characteristic of "Indian" philosophical traditions that is so specific about it or is internal to it? Whatever it may be, this much is clear that "Indian-ness" cannot be defined as a certain homogeneous category – this is evident from the history of this tradition as it has developed in South Asia. This term needs to be defined in its heterogeneity. In fact, one should be sceptical about calling Śaṅkara a Keralite or Malayalee and designating Abhinavagupta as a Kaśmīrī unless one is referring to their ethnic origins taking recourse to the popular traditional beliefs. Kerala and Kashmir are no homogeneous categories either. We have to be aware of this and yet we do have to bring out the contribution of these varied cultural zones as the learned author of this book has done (see the Chapters 7 and 8 in this book). But before we ask any further questions or before we problematize the questions asked by A.K. Ramanujan or Bina Gupta further, we need to ask the fundamental question – in what sense has this term been used in history? What is Indian philosophy and who is an Indian philosopher? What is this label used for? Why does every book on Indian philosophy focus on whatever is available in Sanskrit sources alone? Is "Indian" and Sanskrit synonymous? What is "Hindu" about this philosophy? Can we use "Indian" and "Hindu" interchangeably? How do we solve the problem of "classical" and "contemporary" in case of "Indian philosophy"? Should we use the label "classical Indian philosophy" because often the term "Indian philosophy" does not refer to what one may label as "contemporary Indian thought". But then what is contemporary Indian thought and what relationship does it share with the classical thought in the case of South Asia? Do the labels "traditional" and "modern" solve the problem for us? Are the "traditional" and "modern" categories representing the writings in Sanskrit and English respectively? Is this distinction merely temporal? If someone writes a philosophical text in Sanskrit today, for instance, will it be understood as a traditional or a modern text? Or will it be considered a text belonging to contemporary Indian thought written in a classical language using traditional style? Or will that text be referred to as "original" just because it is written in Sanskrit? Now, taking another instance, if I write a book on Indian philosophy in English, what will that be called? A modern text on traditional philosophy or a traditional text in a modern style? This should allow us to problematize a number of categories those are often taken for granted. All these categories are problematic and they should not be ignored.

Why is it that whatever is called "Indian philosophy" today usually only refers to philosophy in South Asia in its classical sources as if South Asia never moved ahead of the classical age or as if people stopped thinking after the classical age. For instance, as pointed out by Bhushan and Garfield (2017), why is it that we have never paid attention to post-classical philosophical discourses in South Asia? Why have we not examined medieval intellectual histories in non-Sanskritic sources and why have we not analysed the anglophone philosophers writings on "Indian philosophy" in colonial period in South Asia? But this is not the sole issue. In that case, what do we understand by contemporary or modern Indian philosophy? It is very often the case that when one uses the category "modern/contemporary Indian philosophy", we invoke the names of Swami Vivekananda, Mahatma Gandhi, Aurobindo Ghosh, B.R. Ambedkar and others. To add more to this, it is also not very uncommon today to find only Osho or J. Krishnamurty in the sections of "Indian philosophy" in a few popular bookshops in India. Are they modern Indian philosophers? In the contemporary South Asia, who are the practitioners of "Indian philosophy", both traditional and modern?

It should certainly be asked why we have refrained from engaging with the critical insights of K.C. Bhattacharyya about the idea of Absolute when we make an attempt to understand Śaṅkara's concept of *Brahman*? Is it because K.C. Bhattacharyya is not writing in Sanskrit? Or is it because since he is writing in English and thus he is not seen as a part of the tradition that Śaṅkara or Dharmarāja belonged to? Ironically enough, even if Swami Vivekananda did not write anything much in Sanskrit (except a few hymns in praise of his teacher), he is often made to represent "Indian philosophy" globally, and, in fact, there are only a handful of Sanskritists or contemporary Indian philosophers who are even aware of the solid contribution of K.C. Bhattacharyya to

Indian philosophy. Indian philosophy certainly has been subjected to very vague generalizations on the basis of the popular culture. One of the best examples of this is how Śaṅkara's rigour of making sense of empirical through epistemological investigation has been reduced down to a simplistic and dismal notion of *māyā*. Or how Swami Vivekananda made use of many Vedāntic textual sources to appropriate his quest for ascetic nationalism even though he was not at all unique in doing so. Indian intellectual history, written either in vernacular or cosmopolitan languages like Sanskrit or English, unfortunately, has largely been shaped by the popular discourse. Many such questions resonate in the concerns of Bhushan and Garfield (2017) and also in the anthology edited by Sharad Deshpande (2015).

Invoking another question posed by A.K. Ramanujan "Is there *an* Indian way of thinking?" would then mean asking if there is a linear way of thinking that can be called "Indian". This sounds like an oxymoron in itself. In any given culture there can never be only one way of thinking, but there can be only one way of representing it because of certain historical trajectories. The ontology of the concept of culture is heterogeneity. In case of South Asia this heterogeneity has been strongly practised at the linguistic level as well. I think we have never taken the language question as seriously as we should have in the context of "Indian philosophy". This problem is not related to Sanskrit, Persian and English alone, the problem is related to all the linguistic mediums of intellectual pursuit in South Asia. After all, philosophy in South Asia, for instance, to involve the instrumentality of languages, was not written in Sanskrit alone. It was, as Jonardon Ganeri (2017: 1, Introduction) would maintain, also "written in many languages including Pāli, Prākṛt, Sanskrit, Malayalam, Urdu, Gujarati, Tamil, Telugu, Bengali, Marathi, Persian, Kannada, Punjabi, Hindi, Tibetan, Arabic, and Assamese. From the time of the British colonial occupation, it has also been written in English." Or to go a step ahead and ask the question why is it that every discourse or any textbook on "Indian philosophy" ends up introducing or examining the Sanskrit sources alone as if there were no "patterns of thinking" being discussed in other South Asian languages. Even within the domains of each one of these linguistic cultures, there has been heterogeneity of thought, subject matter and approach. It is not that the Sanskrit sources "are" hegemonic as they are often said to be, but we have supplied this hegemony to them very generously. And we have also done this rather by neglecting the non-Sanskrit sources for too long. In fact, the Sanskrit sources themselves are hardly explored properly and many a time terribly misinterpreted in the popular discourse as mentioned above. One of the important examples of this negligence is that except P.V. Kane no one has really seriously studied socio-political thought in pre-modern South Asia and brought it on the table for critical evaluation. Much of the unpopular Dharmaśāstric literature still lies in the dismal dungeons of manuscript libraries in India. And may I add Tāntric literature to this league. Indeed there is Sanskrit literature that is treated as subaltern, that at least needs to be gazed at in order to look at the Indian intellectual history afresh.

Another important issue is that we have hardly even explored the meaning of this "Indian-ness" in all its differentiated forms. It is again very recently that scholars have begun to explore the philosophy of aesthetics in South Asia or what it means for various cultures in different times, or where at least in pre-modern South Asia lay the distinction between what is literary and philosophical. In other words what is qualified as literature or what is constituted of philosophy? Or to ask if there was at all a stark distinction between the two categories! How were the logical–epistemological structural paradigms, as pointed out in several chapters by the author in this book, not only influencing the discourse on poetry and poetics, but also shaping them up very subtly (see the Chapters 4, 9 and 12 in the present book). To use the structural terminology – how Buddhist concepts helped shaping Hindu ideas and how Hindu ideas influenced the Buddhist concepts, or how both added up to form new structures or concepts altogether (see the Chapters 10 and 11 in the present book). Citing Ganeri (2017: 2, Introduction) it is also important to ask if, in pre-modern South Asia there was no "important philosophical thinking among mathematicians and medics, in the poets and the pilgrims, while studies of philosophy in sūfī India, secular India and stately India, of India's impact on global philosophical movements, and their effects on India all fall within the remit, not to mention the way Indian philosophical ideas migrate and transform in diaspora, in Nepal, Sri Lanka, Burma, Tibet, Thailand, Indonesia, Cambodia, China, Japan, Central Asia and into the Persian and Arabic worlds and on to the West." This cannot be ignored. In fact, it is only recently that scholars have started to explore the non-Sanskrit philosophical traditions of South Asia. One only needs to take an example from Perso-Arabic sources or the interaction thereof with Sanskrit. As Ganeri (2017: 8, Introduction) further says:

> Three important Islamic trends in India emerge during the seventeenth and eighteenth centuries: first, the Perso-Indica project of Dārā Shikuh and others involving a wide-ranging translation of philosophy from Sanskrit into Persian; second, the sūfī philosophy of Muḥibballāh Ilāhābādī, a prolific author in Persian and Arabic and defender of the Andalusian Ibn 'Arabī; and third, the debate between Avicennans – notably including the influential philosopher Maḥmūd Jawnpūrī – and Illuminationists. Meanwhile, Muḥibballāh al-Bihārī's *Sullam al-'ulūm* is a milestone seventeenth-century Indian textbook in Arabo-Islamic logic. We still have only the most rudimentary understanding of the nature of intersections between nodes of Sanskrit, Persian, and Arabic philosophical scholarship during this profoundly innovative era of early modernity in India. Nor at present do we have much insight into the dynamics of philosophical activity in Indian vernacular languages in the period.

The above questions need to be asked – they need to be asked because they are unasked questions and we need to develop "new formulations of old insights". One should stop making claims and begin asking questions. Not that older philosophers and scholars did not, but looking into the background of these questions and question the question itself? (see Daya Krishna, pp. 29ff in

Bhushan and Garfield 2011) "So, one not only has to question the traditions but question the old ways of questioning them." Or to quote Arindam Chakrabarti:

> To anticipate our conclusion, it would transpire that the real novelty of philosophical thinking lies in seeing new – in the epistemic sense of hitherto unperceived – connections between apparently unconnected conceptual questions or muddles, rather than in creating new concepts.
>
> – Chakrabarti (p. 5) in Bhushan and Garfield 2011

But apart from this what also needs to be asked is – is there only one way of approaching Indian philosophy? Can any thinking pattern function in cultural isolation, no matter how rigid it has been over the course of its development in history. Is it not going to influence the social or political or literary or linguistic practices outside its own domain one way or the other or will it not itself get influenced by these practices other than its own irrespective of the fact whether it does or does not ever come in a very close proximity with parallel thinking practices elsewhere in the world owing to various historical trajectories? Who can prevent this? Or why should one prevent this at all? Should this change be considered as a creative development in that thinking tradition or should it be considered interfering with the pure nature of it? Who should get to decide it? And the most compelling question – are we as the meaning makers not a part of this project, i.e. is the understanding of reader/listener/receiver of such traditions also not a part of this thinking tradition?

In the South Asian context it is not at all difficult to observe a fathomless void between its past and its present (see Raghuramaraju 2011). Was this fathomless isolation manufactured by the presence of colonialism? Tradition and modernity, complex terms as they are in the South Asia context, do possess a significant contrast. This contrast needs to be carefully understood. One layer of this contrast is the dichotomy of spiritual and material, and these terms are artfully synchronized with Eastern and Western philosophies respectively. As if, as Daya Krishna would say, no one thought about "matter" in the East or there was no spirituality in the West. On the one hand I have been saying that we should learn how to create a narrative that is beyond the dichotomies of the East and the West, yet at the same time this is also true that a book on Western philosophy does not necessarily need to be approached through post-colonial method (see Richard King 1999b). This, on the other hand, would be absolutely important in the case of "Indian philosophy". And this has to be done for a number of reasons. These pre-modern traditions are to be strictly understood on their own terms, but at the same time meaningful and serious comparative interaction cannot be ruled out. In the world we live in today, we cannot afford to be frogs in the well. We have to be able to bring in the large picture of South Asian intellectual cultures on a wide canvas where we can portray its universal picture in comparison to various other grand intellectual cultures of the world. This cannot be compromised for any other petty concerns those of, either insiders or outsiders, the discipline may hold.

Predominantly, the scholars who study "Indian philosophy" are of two broad categories. One type of scholars are those who usually do not engage with original Sanskrit sources using philological methods. These scholars may mostly depend on the secondary sources or translations of the primary texts. Some of them may be more interested in comparative philosophy and some may be well grounded in theoretical models or methods, but lacking awareness of various cultural zones and their patterns of practising thinking consciousness. The question is that if one is a well-trained philosopher in studying methodological patterns, why should s/he not be able to understand the philosophical concerns of any other cultural zone even if s/he is not completely aware of that cultural entity itself. One may lack in a few objective pieces of information, but it is not impossible to engage with it. For instance, all philosophical queries have to have epistemological concerns. They will have concerns about ethics and aesthetics, social and political. What the concerns are and how they are understood may, of course, vary. This must also be pointed out that occasionally such scholars do make grave philological mistakes that can really make the whole philosophical edifice vulnerable. Indeed I feel the need of quoting Sheldon Pollock (2011: 37-38) emphasizing the importance of philology:

> This discipline of making sense of texts, which I have been talking about here all along, is what used to be called – and what I hope will one day again be called, with pride – philology. Philology is central to all reading, whether that of a Sangam poet or a Dalit novelist, though it seems to confront us as a methodological issue in direct proportion to the distance in time and space that separates us from the text. We naively think the contemporary text transparently accessible, but making sense of it always requires philology, which becomes more effective the more present it is to our consciousness. Learning a classical language renders philology permanently present; it enables us to read with sustained discipline, teaching us above all to distinguish and balance the three core domains of meaning: the author's, the tradition's, and, most important, our own.

From Pollock above, it is clear that another league of scholars is who use philological methods and strongly depend upon the original textual sources. I, of course, do not deny that one cannot find a fine blend of a philologist and a philosopher. In fact, I do also agree that one cannot do good philosophy without doing good philology. The problem, however, is that in some cases philologists end up being mere slaves of a text. They do not understand the meaning of philology in the same catholic sense as Pollock is mentioning. They would know the text perfectly well but anything outside the domain of the text and the textual tradition is redundant for them. Let us take the example of traditional Śāstric scholars, who are not only well trained in the Sanskrit language, but also practise pedagogical methods of philosophizing about these Śāstras. While many philosophers have often engaged with the discourses based on secondary scholarship available to them, i.e. translations and studies often in languages other than Sanskrit, many other scholars, particularly Śāstric scholars have many a time not even seen these books written in languages other than Sanskrit. To illustrate, in some situations, if I have introduced a traditionally trained scholar to someone like Daya Krishna or Jonardon Ganeri (or in other cases I have also given K.C. Bhattacharyya a try), the students audaciously replied back saying they were not interested in "such stuff". On the other hand, whenever I tried getting students who are trained in modern pedagogy interested in traditional methods or philological approach or the importance of a text, in the majority of cases their reply was nothing different – they were also not interested in "such stuff". I often wonder why couldn't there be a Daya Krishna or a K.C. Bhattacharyya in dialogue (virtually or in reality) with Mani Dravida Shastri or vice versa. Both seem to have exactly same concerns at a very abstract level. They function on the same platform, pursuing exactly the same engagement with the same texts, theories, studies, etc. yet they strictly live in the two different worlds – modern and pre-modern – and ironically both these worlds do remain located in the contemporary. Kalidas Bhattacharyya blames the old school scholars saying:

> The difficulty with these old-type scholars in Indian philosophy is that they live in a self-contained world of their own and do not care to communicate with others except in their own limited world. ... This was the state of affairs even in the old-day India.
> – Kalidas Bhattacharyya as quoted in Raghuramaraju 2006: 3

While I do not disagree with Bhattacharyya, I do think that this process has to be mutual. Both parties have to step forward. We as classically trained scholars do also have to learn how to pose modern questions. Unfortunately, the modern relevance of the classical world, specifically in case of South Asia, has remained confined merely to its glorification and not learning from it. This "continuing seclusion" between the past and present, as Bhattacharyya warns us and as we are able to witness it at present in India, "could only lead to 'inbreeding in the field of ideas', and this would be only 'false patriotism and harmful nostalgia'" (Raghuramaraju 2006: 4). This is why Elise Coquereau-Saouma and Elisa Freschi (2018) ask a question in case of post-colonial philosophy in India in the form of the subtitle of a journal – "Too Alien for Contemporary Philosophers, Too Modern for Sanskritists?". Their concern is reflected in the following words:

> [Contemporary Indian philosophy] is marked by a widespread instruction in English focusing on "Western" philosophy, reinterpreted in an Indian context, as opposed to a traditional Sanskrit-based learning. This situation, inherited from colonial times, is combined among contemporary Indian philosophers with an awareness of the gap and a reflection on the consequences of colonization on Indian philosophy, characterizing the "postcolonial" era. A first demand for accessing the global academic discourse was formulated by Indian philosophers in terms of similarity to show that Indian philosophy is philosophical, thereby equal to "Western" philosophy. This demand is followed by a search for identity vis-à-vis the local academic discourse in terms of authenticity if Indian philosophy is conceptualized in English. We therefore addressed issues related to the transition from the colonial external influences to the postcolonial internal developments that contribute to characterizing the cultural and linguistic plurality of Indian philosophical traditions.
>
> – Coquereau-Saouma and Freschi 2018: 358

There is another significant dimension related to the question of languages that is often terribly neglected by us. It is related to the pragmatics of the functionality of languages in the context of Indian philosophical discourse. We often do not realize how important is this question of language in terms of either the accessibility of the original source material or whether interpreting or translating or engaging with it in the languages like English and Hindi. Quoting Talal Asad, Richard King (1999a: 237-38) places an emphasis on the idea of "the inequality of languages" while discussing the ideas of translation. He says that languages from the Third World societies are more likely to succumb to a "forcible transformation" when they are translated into Western languages. In his view the opposite is less likely as languages from Third

World societies are often seen as "weaker" when compared to a First World Western language. His observations reflect a larger problem – when a text is being translated, there will always be certain words that cannot be translated accurately as the meaning those words hold has no cultural equivalent in the language into which it is being translated. Often times the European translation does not reflect this limitation in the way the text is written. This leads to the translation being overly Anglicized it tends to "obscure and subordinate differences" (King 1999a: 237). In addition to this, it is deemed acceptable, however if a translation of a text from English into an Indian language is overly "Indianized", for example, it may not be as respected as an overly Anglicized translation of an Indian text (also see Bhushan and Garfield 2011).

The question of language is also important because for many scholars, who are seriously interested in the discourse on Indian philosophy, do not either have access to original sources or they do not have the possibility of having a dialogue with Śāstric scholars. Of course, the question is also whether many of the secondary sources discussing original thoughts and concerns are available in languages other than English. How many critically acclaimed and highly focused books on Indian philosophy are written, translated or simply available in Urdu, Malayalam, Kannada, Bengali, Kashmiri, etc.? In a few cases, where such examples are available, they are not given appropriate credit that they deserve. They are simply ignored as if they never existed. Very often South Asian scholars do not write critical essays in South Asian languages other than English (not that English is not a South Asian language). If critical thinking is possible in English, it should be possible in other South Asian languages as well. As Navjivan Rastogi told me once that he began focusing more on writing in Hindi not because he did not have the choice of writing in English or other languages he knows, but he wanted to write in Hindi owing to his resilience that displays that critical scholarship is possible in Hindi as well. Unfortunately, we also have some very popular but bad specimens of introductory books on Indian philosophy in Hindi, for instance the books titled the *Bhāratīya Darśana kī Rūparekhā* (1979) and *Bhāratīya Darśana* (1976) by Baladeva Upadhyaya. These books have been very popular amongst Sanskrit students even while they are absolutely uncritical specimens of scholarship. In comparison to this, in the recent scholarship, Navjivan Rastogi's *Abhinavagupta kā Tantrāgamīya Darśana* (2018) and *Kāśmīra Śivādvayavāda maiṅ Pramāṇa-cintana* (2013) and Ambikadatta Sharma's *Bauddha Pramāṇa Darśana* (2016) are certainly the best specimens of critical scholarship on Indian thought in Hindi language. No one can deny this fact that today the most critical scholarship on Indian philosophy is available in English language. Of course, English has international presence and no one should have problems with this. But this is also a fact that traditionally-trained teachers and students usually do not have access to this scholarship in English language for a number of reasons. So how can we answer the question – why should a traditional *paṇḍit* who is otherwise well versed in the Sanskrit texts of Indian philosophy read the books of Jonardon Ganeri or Stephen Phillips to use an illustration? The other side of the problem is that the traditional Sanskrit scholars are usually inclined towards oral scholarship than the written scholarship. And how many traditional Sanskrit scholars either read or care to read books about their subject in English. But then how many modern scholars of classical Indian philosophy who mostly write in English care about the original views (even if only available in oral) of the traditional scholars of Indian philosophy either.

This allows me to claim that no debate on Indian philosophy is ever possible without using post-colonial theory and orientalism. This is not obviously the case with Western philosophy, for instance. Much has already been said about the impact of colonialism on the South Asian mind. I may only reiterate what others have said – in what different ways did colonialism impact South Asian mind and how can such patterns be understood using post-colonial models. The presence of Western philosophy and the severity of its impact on South Asia is reflected upon by Kalidas Bhattacharyya thus:

> Most of the others who have not done philosophy in India

> since have more or less severely accepted Western philosophy, and that too as it was understood by the British thinkers, and granted recognition to the much only of Indianism which was intelligible, in terms of Western ideas. The rest was rejected as dogmatic, magical, tribal, romantic, speculative and what not?
>
> – Kalidas Bhattacharyya as quoted in Raghuramaraju 2006 :3

The question to be asked is how was philosophy functioning as a discipline from within and without in South Asia itself. In other words, how was thinking being practised in South Asia itself, how was it being analysed by South Asians themselves and how different was this from the analysis of the one who studied South Asia from outside South Asia. I use the categories like "insider" and "outsider" via-à-vis the discipline of Indian philosophy. Richard King raises the question if we can study Indian philosophy with a decontextualized approach (King 1999a: 24-26). Is there a universal way of thinking? Are there universal parameters of rationality? And is rationality the only parameter of philosophy? Oriental thought was often accused by colonial Indologists as stagnant and unchanging while they were looking for a homogeneous category called "Indian-ness" that was propelled by attempts of trying to fit a model where the reference point was the West (Raghuramaraju 2006: 6).

This perspective subtly also permeated into the minds of the South Asian scholars of the late nineteenth and the early twentieth century. Scholars like S. Radhakrishnan emphasized the idea of Indian philosophy being spiritual centred while scholars like B.K. Matilal and J.N. Mohanty emphasized the reason and logic and scholars like Debi Prasad Chattopadhyay emphasized the material component (Raghuramaraju 2006: 11ff). The discourse on Indian philosophy has also thrived through many such biases. There are thinkers according to whom Indian philosophy, and thus Indian mind, was virtually destroyed by colonial intervention. Daya Krishna, who warns us against the possibility of Indian philosophy remaining merely a subject of antiquarian interest and research, characterizes the present picture of Indian philosophy as "dead and mummified" (Krishna 1991: 15) (see also the discussion by Raghuramaraju (2006: 6ff) on this). When A.K. Ramanujan is asking the question – *Is* there an Indian way of thinking? – he can be understood referring to what Daya Krishna often complained about, i.e. whatever one may call "Indian philosophy" has always been contextualized as a historical category – a fossilized idea where nothing is encouraged except understanding the philosophy as a historical category in the museum of time and eternity. Did Indian philosophy, as argued by Daya Krishna, really die during the colonial era? According to Raghuramaraju (2006: 7) Daya Krishna's comment actually gives too much credit to colonialism and indeed the recent work of Bhushan and Garfield (2017) has exemplified this. They have proven it wrong that the Indian philosophy was only "improvement in style, and not in substance" (Raghuramaraju 2006).

There is no introductory book on "Indian philosophy" published in the past couple of decades that does not begin with a discourse on "Can there Be Philosophy in India?" or "What Is Indian about Philosophy?" or "Is There an Indian Way of Thinking?". Why is it that each time a scholar doing Indian philosophy needs to justify to what Indian philosophy is, what it constitutes of and why should it be there at all? Or does it qualify to be philosophy at all at the first place? This is also true that this question has now been over-exhausted in some sense because a lot has been said, thought and written about it and philosophers seem to have overcome the limitation of "Indian-ness". Now one is to ask bigger questions: Do we need to write a fresh critical history of Indian philosophy that takes into consideration all such questions raised above? But the idea of attempting a fresh history is neither new nor is it in itself unproblematic. What should this history be of – i.e. should it be a history of philosophical schools, history of philosophers, history of ideas, etc.? But this all need to be written or rewritten in a fashion where we are keeping in mind a number of elements, viz. what in many ways we have been familiarized with, strictly speaking, is not what Indian philosophy is. Many of the misnomers and misunderstandings created on the basis of some kind of homogeneity of thought and narrative have been canonized as the story of Indian philosophy.

As the author of this book is carefully reflecting upon the individual contributions of Śaṅkara and Paṇḍitarāja Jagannātha, we should not ignore the individual contribution of Indian philosophers who have been often studied only restricted to the strict traditional boundaries that they have belonged to. As Daya Krishna said:

> [The schools of Indian philosophy] are treated as something finished and final. No distinction, therefore, is ever made between the thought of an individual thinker and the thought of a school. A school is, in an important sense, an abstraction. It is a logical construction springing out of the writings of a number of thinkers who share a certain similarity of outlook in tackling certain problems. Sāṁkhya, for example, is identified too much with Īśvarakṛṣṇa's work, or Vedānta with the work of Śaṅkara. But this is due to a confusion between the thought of an individual thinker and the style of thought which he exemplifies and to which he contributes in some manner. All that Śaṅkara has written is not strictly Advaita Vedānta. Nor all that Īśvarakṛṣṇa has written, Sāṁkhya. Unless this is realized, writings on Indian philosophy will continuously do injustice either to the complexity of thought of the individual thinker concerned, or to the uniqueness of the style they are writing about. – Krishna 1991: 14

This has been further clarified by Andrew Nicholson (2010) elucidating that the diversity of thoughts found in different schools of Indian philosophical tradition, alongside dispelling modern notions concerning Śaṅkara's Advaita Vedānta as the ultimate essence of "Hindu" thought. Nicholson has argued against this understanding of Hinduism based on Orientalist's imagination, motivated by colonialist's intention to structurally appropriate and classify diverse Indian philosophical traditions. This Euro-centric approach in classifying and interpreting selective Indian philosophical texts, Nicholson says, failed to take into consideration the evolving nature of Indian philosophical traditions, and often undermined the significant role played by premodern Indian doxographers like Vijñānabhikṣu and Madhusūdana Sarasvatī who wrote commentaries on foundational texts or Sūtras of other schools; and in their attempt hierarchically classified them on the basis of levels of reality and unified Āstika schools.

Further, the reuse or adaptive reuse of ideas or the deeply penetrating influence of one individual philosopher or the tradition s/he belongs to over the other philosophers or their traditions converge into forming the building blocks of developing these thinking systems. We should study the trajectory of Indian philosophy in such a way where we should feel compelled to engage with the questions like why did Cārvākas die out and Vedāntins flourish? We should focus more on the criticality of ideas. How is the dualism of Sāṁkhya evolving towards the non-binary principle of non-duality represented by an absolute category called *Brahman*, yet at the same time compromising with the idea of *māyā*? How was Śaṅkara achieving this aim in the ninth century CE and how was Dharmarāja fulfilling it in the seventeenth century CE? How was Śrīharṣa practising "contrary thinking" in the twelfth century CE to strengthen the same concept of non-duality further? How was Abhinavagupta doing it in the eleventh century CE where once again the duality between the subject and the object in the form of Śiva and Śakti or knower and known was compromised with a master stroke? Or if we had to imagine Abhinavagupta who was not preceded by Bhartṛhari, Ānandavardhana and Dharmakīrti? Or can we imagine the commentator Abhinavagupta without his grand-master Utpaladeva? Can we imagine today the Theory of Rasa without Abhinavagupta's contribution? Or what would have been the scenario of Indian philosophical landscape if Gaṅgeśopādhyāya had not brought in the Navya-Nyāya revolution in the late twelfth century CE? The question is if the philosophical creativity of the Śaiva and Vaiṣṇava philosophers lied in adding eleven more ontological categories (*tattvas*) to the Sāṁkhya model of Ontology, where does our philosophical creativity lie? Just by knowing about it? Or merely by pointing this out, etc.

cannot qualify for philosophizing about it. Even the Sanskrit commentarial tradition itself, as pointed out by Jonardon Ganeri (2010), has been extremely critical about it, then how can we afford to be mindlessly uncritical about it:

> ... a successful philosophical commentary helps its target audience to read philosophically the text being commented upon, and mediates between the text and a given readership. Potentially, the features which mark out a text as being a valuable work of philosophy might include coherence and completeness in the description of a point of view, sound argument in favour of the view described, engagement with alternative views, demonstration of the utility of the view in question, and so on. At later times or in other cultural communities, new audiences can approach a philosophical commentary as a window through which to see what the practice of philosophical reading has meant to others. – Ganeri 2010: 187

This is what C. Rajendran has achieved in this book. The short, laconic and precise essays are a philosophical commentary on several select themes those he has deemed essential and worthy of speculation. In order to do this, as argued by Daya Krishna and also by the present author in the very first chapter of the book, we must explore the possibility of developing a fresh model of comparative philosophy:

> "Comparative studies", thus, meant in effect the comparison of all other societies and cultures in terms of the standards provided by the Western societies and cultures both in cognitive and non-cognitive domains. The scholars belonging to these other societies and cultures, instead of looking at Western society and culture from their own perspectives, accepted the norms provided by Western scholars and tried to show that the achievements in various fields within their cultures paralleled those in the West and thus they could not be regarded as inferior in any way to those which were found there. This hindered the emergence of what may be called "comparative 'comparative studies'" which might have led to a more balanced perspective in these fields. – Krishna 1989: 59-60

Comparative models could be dangerous, even harmful if no perfect justice is done to what is being compared and with what it is being compared. Comparative model should argue for developing a method that is not an indigenous method delimited by its "Indian-ness", but is a theoretically abstract method that argues for a robust presentation of what one may call Indian philosophy. A strong warning with subtle concern for how comparative models should be approached and executed in the case of South Asia comes from A. Raghuramaraju:

> So, there is a need to build the various protocols of scholarship and convert these writers into authors, and then embark on comparisons. We need to first prepare the writings of Gandhi or Ambedkar by making them systematic, before we relate them or compare them either with Derrida or Benjamin. Directly comparing some ideas of these thinkers from India with established philosophers such as Derrida or Benjamin will not yield the intended results. All this involves getting the material ready. There is a difference between using ready-made academic material and preparing it first and then use it. Most often, in Indian universities, the readily available academic resources of Euro-American philosophy are used thus leading to Euro-centric teaching. Correspondingly, there has not been concerted efforts to make Indian writers and philosophers writings made ready. There is a variance, unevenness, between these two. I am sensitive to this and wish to tread carefully so as not to accentuate the difference or unevenness. Unlike in the Euro-American world, in India, academic resources are not available ready-made, one has to get them ready for use. This is a long procedure, and it requires different levels, stages, and methods of preparation. Firstly, the resources have to be identified and their descriptions have to be drawn up. One, then, needs to find out if there are existing interpretations available on them, and write about these realities, practices, or ideas in a new idiom. Only then, these can be used in academic discussions. Directly using the resources from India can expose these scholars from India to vulnerabilities and render them less enduring – to be considered esoteric at most, attracting more of curiosity than

> academic credibility, despite themes and ideas from India gaining visibility at the global level.
> – Raghuramaraju p. 476 in Coquereau-Saouma and Freschi 2018

Understanding Raghuramaraju's concern for making Indian writers and philosophers writings ready for comparison also applies to all Sanskrit philosophers. While comparisons are a way ahead to unpack the denseness of many tersely packed concepts, I still believe we first need to attempt to trace the ideas in themselves and map their clear territories in history. An excellent example of this is presented by David Shulman in his *More than Real: A History of the Imagination in South India* (2012) wherein he lucidly and yet impenetrably maps a territory of the idea of imagination for us (also see Bhushan and Garfield (2017: 20ff) on this). Shulman's this work should certainly stand as a model example for us.

Professor C. Rajendran is a literary craftsman of a rare disposition who combines in himself a fine philosopher and philologist and we must learn from his lifelong scholarship of a matchless teacher and dedicated man of letters. His provocative insights sharing penetrative acumen both in his traditional and modern approaches to South Asian intellectual systems is an inspiration for many of us particularly when, unfortunately, much of South Asian Sanskrit scholarship is preoccupied creating stark and dismal distinctions between the scholars from both East and West, traditional and modern. I feel terribly sad when I see even some of the veteran Sanskrit scholars in South Asia succumbing to the misleading concerns of South Asian diaspora in the Western countries that eventually gives rise to what Kalidas Bhattacharyya called "false patriotism and harmful nostalgia". Fossilized minds of the South Asian diaspora only cater to their insecured obsessions and grave preoccupation of losing their identity and they try to exercise their so-called intellectual capital to innocent scholars in India misleading them to this notion that they are being misrepresented in the West or by the Western scholars of Sanskrit. As Rajendran himself says that there are "bad" scholars both in the East and the West, and in the same way there are "good" scholars both in the East and the West.

We cannot afford to leave even the traces of "bad" and terrible scholarship to Sanskrit students I was talking about towards the beginning of this essay. They should be guided by their own critical acumen and questioning minds rather than this unceasing urge of protecting and glorifying what they study. They should practice "Contrary Thinking".

References

Bhushan, N. and D. Raveh (eds), 2011, *Contrary Thinking: Selected Essays of Daya Krishna*, New York: Oxford University Press.

Bhushan, N. and J.L. Garfield (eds), 2011, *Indian Philosophy in English from Renaissance to Independence*, New York: Oxford University Press.

———, 2017, *Minds Without Fear: Philosophy in the Indian Renaissance*, New York: Oxford University Press.

Coquereau-Saouma, Elise and Elisa Freschi (guest eds), 2018, *Sophia*, 57(3), September, Special Issue on The Challenge of Postcolonial Philosophy in India: Too Alien for Contemporary Philosophers, Too Modern for Sanskritists.

Deshpande, Sharad (ed.), 2015, *Philosophy in Colonial India* (*Sophia*, Studies in Cross-cultural Philosophy of Traditions and Cultures, 11), Delhi: Springer India.

Ganeri, Jonardon, 2010, "Sanskrit Philosophical Commentary", *Journal of the Indian Council of Philosophical Research*, 27: 187-207.

Ganeri, Jonardon (ed.), 2017, *Oxford Handbook of Indian Philosophy*, New York: Oxford University Press.

Gupta, Bina, 2012, *An Introduction to Indian Philosophy: Perspectives on Reality, Knowledge, and Freedom*, New York: Routledge.

King, Richard, 1999a, *Indian Philosophy: An Introduction to Hindu and Buddhist Thought*, Edinburg: Edinburg University Press.

———, 1999b, *Orientalism and Religion: Post-Colonial Theory, India and "The Mystic East"*, New York: Routledge.

Krishna, Daya, 1989, "Comparative Philosophy: What It Is and What It Ought to Be", in *Interpreting Across Boundaries: New Essays in Comparative Philosophy*, ed. Gerald James Larson and Eliot Deutsch,

Delhi: Motilal Banarsidass (repr.: Princenton University Press, 2014).

———, 1991, *Indian Philosophy: A Counter Perspective*, New Delhi: Oxford University Press.

Nicholson, Andrew J., 2010, *Unifying Hinduism: Philosophy and Identity in Indian Intellectual History*, New York: Columbia University Press.

Perrett, Roy W., 2016, *An Introduction to Indian Philosophy*, Cambridge: Cambridge University Press.

Pollock, Sheldon, 2011, "Crisis in the Classics", *Social Research*, 78(1): 21-48.

Raghuramaraju, A., 2006, *Debates in Indian Philosophy: Classical, Colonial, and Contemporary*, New Delhi: Oxford University Press.

Raghuramaraju, A., 2011, *Enduring Colonialism: Classical Presences and Modern Absences in Indian Philosophy*, New Delhi: Oxford University Press.

Ramanujan, A.K., 1999, *The Collected Essays of A.K. Ramanujan*, ed. Vinay Dharwadker, New Delhi: Oxford University Press.

Rastogi, Navjivan, 2018, *Abhinavagupta kā Tantrāgamīya Darśana*, 2nd rev. edn, New Delhi: D.K. Printworld.

Sharma, Ambika Datta, 2016, *Bauddha Pramāṇa Darśana: Pramāṇaśāstrīya Siddhāntoṅ kā Adhiprāmāṇya Viśleṣaṇa*, rev. and enlarged edn, New Delhi: D.K. Printworld.

Shulman, David D., 2012, *More than Real: A History of the Imagination in South India*, Cambridge, MA: Harvard University Press.

Preface

CLASSICAL Indian philosophy seems to have many points worth exploring despite the impressive scholarly inputs accumulated over the years. The papers collected in the present volume are the outcome of my own occasional engagements with such issues, related to its history, impact, epistemology and hermeneutics. These were either written for special occasions or presented in seminars. Some of them are surveys and influence studies; some address the interface between philosophy and poetics; some deal with methodological and epistemological issues. The introductory study is related to problems of comparative philosophy which has to take off in a big way in years to come.

I am greatly obliged to Mrinal Kaul, my young friend and a distinguished scholar of international repute, who has kindly offered to write an Introduction to this collection. Mrinal's passion for philosophy is contagious and his gentle persuasion has been a constant source of inspiration for me to prepare this collection. I am deeply indebted to Mr Susheel Mittal, who has readily taken up the work for publication. Mr Mittal has consistently maintained international standards in Indological publications and it is a matter of pride to me that I can also join the august company of authors under the rubrics of D.K. Printworld.

Rajendran C.

Contents

1

Comparative Philosophy
Problems and Approaches

COMPARATIVE philosophy, which is to be systematically demarcated from comparative studies of culture, language, politics and other human discourses in content and methodology, is regarded as the philosophy of philosophies (Raju 1970: Preface). Its method is comparison; material, philosophical thought; and outcome, a global discourse of philosophical thought cutting across creeds and nations. The *Internet Encyclopedia of Philosophy* describes comparative philosophy as "a subfield of philosophy in which philosophers work on problems by intentionally setting into dialogue various sources from across cultural, linguistic, and philosophical streams". Accordingly, "the ambition and challenge of comparative philosophy are to include all the philosophies of global humanity in its vision of what is constituted by philosophy". The term cross-cultural philosophy, used as its synonym, gives us an idea of its range and extent. It has the ambitious agenda of being an inclusive discourse comprising and subsuming all philosophical thought of the globe. Yet, however laudable are the aims and objectives of it, there has been some introspection about its achievements and reception from many quarters in the last decades. In 1992, B.K. Matilal confessed that comparative philosophy has had a bad reputation, and the reason for this may be the failure and lack of depth of early comparativists.

Comparative philosophy is often spoken of in an apologetic tone by the protagonists and accepted at best with a patronizing manner by the mainstream philosophers who are not simply interested in cross-cultural dialogues. For that matter, even comparative literature which has made global inroads has been charged as lacking in methodology. But before laying blame squarely on the incompetence of the protagonists of comparative philosophy, I would like to point out that the situation is far more complex and that there are very many reasons for the retarded state of comparative studies in philosophy though I would also like to add that things are changing for the better more than two decades after Matilal had made his critical remark. One of the reasons for the alleged failure on the part of earlier comparativists to take off in a big way is the deep-rooted prejudices regarding alien philosophies held by otherwise eminent philosophers who were either unwilling or incapable of looking at other thought systems with an open mind. It will be important to review early attempts to find out the assumptions, methodology, reception and limitations of earlier attempts to have a proper historical and critical perspective.

Earlier attempts in comparative philosophy had lofty aims like producing unity of meaning and purpose of life with reference to a comprehensive system of values. Despite rooted prejudices and scepticism voiced from traditional quarters, comparativists shared a certain excitement and euphoria about their mission and vision in a world no longer divided into traditional boundaries. Most of them shared the belief that earlier cross-cultural encounters were a far cry from the methodological discipline with which comparative philosophy was to be armoured in solving complex issues. Writing in 1970, P.T. Raju, one of the earlier proponents of comparative philosophy in the last century locates the genesis of comparative philosophy to the cultural context where the East and West were merging both violently and non-violently with each other. Raju claims that it belongs to the twentieth century and believed that it was the most philosophical activity of the present. The instances cited by him of earlier inadequate attempts include the interface between Buddhism and Taoism in China in the first centuries of the Christian era and that of Vedāntic thought and post-Kantian idealist thought in Germany. Even though alien philosophies like those of China have been scrutinized by philosophers like Hegel, such cursory treatment lacks the required depth for want of serious engagement in the dialogue by the non-Western counterparts like the Chinese. In Asia the tradition is somewhat different. The migration of Buddhist thought from India to places like China, Korea, Japan, Sri Lanka, Thailand and Vietnam resulted in meaningful dialogues between indigenous tradition and Buddhism. In China, philosophical history is characterized by the interface between Buddhism on one hand and Confucianism and Taoism on the other. However, there have been a lot of problems caused by linguistic and other cultural factors in the migration and assimilation of alien thought in many countries in the transmission of systems like Buddhism. Thus logic is a blind spot in Japanese Buddhism as the sophisticated Buddhist logic is difficult to translate and discuss in the Japanese language. Logic was practically absent in traditional China also. Coming to modern times, in modern India, the dialogue was initiated by Sri Aurobindo and S. Radhakrishnan. In Japan, Western philosophy was assimilated by a tradition reinforced by Mahāyāna Buddhism.

The projects envisioned by Raju are themselves not free from controversies and ambiguities. There have been a lot of sceptical voices even denying any legitimacy for comparative philosophy as a discipline. Raju records that R.N. Dandekar, a highly respected Indologist, even while chairing one session of series of lectures of the former on comparative philosophy maintained that comparative philosophy is neither possible nor desirable. The reason cited by him for comparison being impossible was that Eastern philosophies like the Indian are spiritual and practical in aim and outlook and Western philosophies are merely intellectual and this-worldly. Of course, such stereotyped perceptions can be refuted, as done by the author himself. It is not correct to designate all Eastern thought as spiritual and all Western thought as materialistic. The second objection seems to be more valid. Dandekar feared that comparison of concepts would result in subordination, presumably of the Eastern by the Western, and not coordination. Of course, there is some danger of a marginalized philosophy being subordinated in any comparative project, but Raju was optimistic of overcoming such dangers as he believed that subordination is not relevant in philosophical discussion. Raju prefers the term "complementing" to denote the project. This is possible when one realizes that one system of philosophy is inadequate by itself and another system will fit in a deeper and wider whole of which the former is a member (Raju 1970: 71). Whether East–West dialogue was conducted in this ideal way is another problem as stereotypes and deeply ingrained prejudices are hard to overcome, as we shall see subsequently.

Raju himself has a clear-cut methodological framework to address the problems inherent in any East–West dialogue. He maintains that the aim of comparative philosophy is to arrive at the unity of meaning and purpose of life with reference to a comprehensive and integrated system of values. He admits that there is no unanimity of opinion with regard to the methodology and aims of comparative philosophy, but this would be understandable given the nature of infancy of the discipline itself. Some of the elements in two streams of philosophy, like logic and philosophies of science and mathematics, are by their very nature universal and hence need not be addressed to. Comparative philosophy should rather focus on the vision of life immanent in different philosophies. Raju cautions against the European approach of viewing comparative philosophy as phenomenology of philosophies, as this would reduce the enquiry to mere sociology of philosophy probing the relation between a philosophy and its social milieu. The concern of the comparativist is humanistic and what is required is an approach which transcends all phenomena we undertake for study.

With regard to problems related to methodology, *Internet*

Encyclopedia of Philosophy describes, following Martha Nussbaum (1997) "some difficulties facing the comparative philosopher", viz. chauvinism, scepticism, incommensurability and perennialism.

- Descriptive chauvinism is that fault which consists in recreating the other tradition in the image of one's own. This is reading a text from another tradition and assuming that it asks the same questions or constructs responses or answers in a similar manner as that one with which one is most familiar.
- Normative chauvinism makes proponents believe that their tradition is best and that "in so far as the others are different, they are inferior or in error".
- Normative scepticism, arguably a scientific and dispassionate attitude to hypotheses without commitment, consists of narrating the views of different philosophies and suspending all judgement about their adequacy. Comparative philosophy, built on the premise that trans-traditional conversation will refine perceptions, however, does not require a suspension of all critical judgement since forming grounds for deciding among views is actually one of the fundamental tasks of comparative philosophy.
- Incommensurability involves the inability to translate some concepts in one tradition into meaning and reference in some other tradition, the fundamental difference of tradition making mutual comprehension impossible, and difference in epistemological assumptions (Wong 1989: 140-59). Since there is no objective decision criterion justifying the preference for one set of claims over another, the task is to empathize with other philosophical tradition as linked to a meaningful and fulfilling life .
- Perennialism is the wrong assumption that philosophical traditions, rather than evolving are, stratified and static and being stuck in such an attitude will deprive the philosopher the opportunity to look at multiple strands in a given tradition.

That concerns raised by scholars like Dandekar are not lone voices is exemplified by the fact that Harold Coward thought he had to begin the first chapter of his interesting work *Derrida and Indian Philosophy* with the following oft-quoted verse of Rudyard Kipling

Oh East is East and West is West
Never the twain shall meet
Till Earth and Sky stand presently at
God's great judgment seat.

– *The Ballad of East and West* ll.1-2

Instead of continuing the mutual caricaturing of East and West, he calls for a willingness to put oneself in the shoes of the other and to see the world through the eyes of the other (Coward 1990: 16). Coward accepts the distinction made by Richard Rorty between the school of rational dialogue and philosophy as "writing" thriving on techniques of paradox and style. Coward works out a strategy to engage Jacques Derrida, one of the main representatives of the "writerly" school with Bhartṛhari, Śaṅkara, Aurobindo and Nāgārjuna. Coward claims that such an engagement, apart from just building a bridgehead between two traditions, helps us to achieve a deeper self understanding "achieved by examining one's own thinking in relation to the thought of the other" (Coward 1990: 148). Thus Coward reinforces the idea that the writing traditions of Western philosophy and Indian philosophy should come together in constructive and critical dialogue, as exemplified by Kipling himself (op. cit., l. 4): "When two strong men stand face to face, though they come from the ends of the world."

Methodological and other problems, again creep up in attempts to compare linguistic philosophies of canonical figures of the East and the West. The seminar proceedings Bhartṛhari *and Wittgenstein,* edited by Sibajiban Bhattacharyya contains several papers written from a comparative perspective comparing the views of Bhartṛhari and Wittgenstein concerning their perspectives on word and sentence. K.J. Shah speaks about the difficulties involved in the task caused by "difference in time, language, approach and perspective" (2002: 9). The comparison, according to him, has only the modest aim to demonstrate the "limitations and possibilities of each of them". Ashok Kelkar confesses that one difficulty in comparing language philosophers like Bhartṛhari and Wittgenstein is that "the problematic they are disposed to select for closer attention in applying their basic insights present a somewhat limited overlap" (2002: 98). Nevertheless, his proposal of a schemata for comparative studies in linguistic philosophy under four heads seems to be interesting as a roadmap to future comparative study in language philosophy.

Recently, Arindam Chakrabarti and Ralph Weber have given a very perceptive account of the state of affairs, challenges and prospects of comparative philosophy in the introduction to the insightfully titled collection of articles, *Comparative Philosophy Without Borders*, edited by them. Describing their project as collaborative philosophical eclecticism, the authors pinpoint the challenges facing comparative philosophy caused by what they describe as "epistemological colonization" which breed some sort of deep prejudices in the Western institutionalized philosophy. Comparative philosophy is all about "the erecting, detecting, smudging and tearing down of borders between borders of philosophical traditions coming from different parts of the world, different time periods, different disciplinary affiliations, and between opposite or distinguishable persuasions". Borders need not be necessarily confined to the broad East–West framework. They exist, not only in between larger entities line Chinese philosophy and European philosophy, and African philosophy, or between Indian and Chinese Buddhism, but even also between knowledge domains like Nyāya and Buddhist philosophy within Indian philosophy and between epistemology, metaphysics and ethics within Western philosophy. Contrary to the belief that comparative philosophy may be at the best a luxury pursued at leisure or the desperate remedy of failed philosophers, the authors demonstrate its sheer inescapability the moment one represents an ancient system of thought in modern idiom, even within one culture and language family.

To revert to the point discussed at the beginning of the paper, it is ironical that even Bimal Matilal himself, who was honest enough to confess the lack of depth of earlier comparativists, despite his "path-breaking work on the logic, ontology and epistemology of negation", was also sidelined by the so-called mainstream votaries of philosophy. Chakrabarti and Weber record that he was given classes on Indian philosophy in the Oxford sub-faculty of philosophy after much initial hesitation (2015: 12). Karl Potter, another great scholar who has done substantial work on analytical philosophy, also had to pay the price for mastering and analysing Indian philosophy as his work on the former came to be sidelined. This type of stereotyping and marginalizing non-European classical philosophy starts from Hegel and persists in the writings of many, like Richard Rorty. From all this one can rightly conclude that the relative cold shoulder accorded to comparative philosophy in its initial stages continues even now and the reason is far more complex than the lack of competence of early scholars. Hopefully, things seem to have changed in recent times and a time may come when what Sheldon Pollock calls "comparison without hegemony" may materialize.

2

Countering Epistemological Scepticism

The Bhāṭṭa View of Counter Argument as Represented in Mānameyodaya

INFERENCE (*anumāna*) is accepted as a means of valid knowledge by almost all systems of Indian philosophy, either orthodox or heterodox, with the rather unexpected exception in the Cārvākas. One would have expected if some die hard idealists like the Mādhyamikas or Advaitins who are generally sceptical of the common-sense view of the external world tried to strike a note of caution in assuming the validity of the means of knowledge like inference. But surprisingly, if we go by the testimony of Mādhava and others, it is the materialist Cārvāka who stubbornly resists any type of knowledge save that which is derived from the sensory organs. The criticism of the Cārvākas is especially directed against inference as a means of valid knowledge if their views as represented in works like *Sarvadarśanasaṁgraha* are genuine. One is surprised by the relative absence of criticism of the validity of verbal knowledge or analogy. Probably the Cārvākas disdainfully refrained from even considering the merits of the arguments supporting such means of valid knowledge, feeling that such questions do not even arise. In the case of inference, they might have been wary of the practice of orthodox logicians who were determined to legitimize concepts like God with the help of analogical reasoning. Be it as it may, Mādhava refers to several ingenious arguments purportedly adduced by the Cārvākas to refute the validity of inference. The Cārvāka throws down his gauntlet by arguing that invariable concomitance, the very precondition for inference rests on very flimsy grounds. At the outset, according to them, it is to be clarified whether invariable concomitance is the relation between particulars or universals. If invariable concomitance is to be restricted to the known or observed particulars, it would be impossible to have any inference concerning unknown or unobserved particulars, as they are not related to the observed particulars. On the other hand, if invariable concomitance is a universal generalization inclusive of all particulars, then there will be nothing new in its knowledge content, as all that is to be known through inference is already known (Sastri 1932: 211). Comparing the logicians to elephants, he contends that they are stuck in the mud of inference: In the case of particulars, there is no uniformity and in the case of universals, inference is reduced to the knowledge of what is already established

> *viśeṣe 'nugamābhāvāt sāmānye siddhasāddhanāt* |
> *anumānabhaṅgapaṅke'smin nimagnā vādidantinaḥ* ||
> – *Sarvadarśanasaṁgraha*, p. 63

In other words, according to the Cārvākas, there is no sufficient ground to believe in the truth of the universal relation arrived through inductive reasoning (Hiriyanna 1994: 189). Even if it is conceded that observation of known facts warrants the assumption of invariable relation between, say, smoke and fire, the Cārvākas contend that there is no guarantee that it will hold good in uninvestigated and unknown cases also. If it is argued that the relation is confined to essential features of universals unrelated to particulars, then inference will cease to be of any practical relevance as particulars are left out. The Cārvākas argue further that the belief in the validity of inference is only a psychological process and no logical certitude can be attached to it. This would explain the difference among rational philosophers themselves concerning even essential matters (Hiriyanna 1994: 190). One big loophole of this ingenious reasoning is that it itself, being arrived at through induction, validates the proposition it wishes to refute, that *vyāpti* (invariable concomitance) is not valid. Nevertheless, the point raised by the Cārvākas is very much pertinent and cannot be lightly brushed aside. It came to haunt Indian epistemological tradition for long. It was a challenge seriously taken up by rival theorists like the Buddhists, Naiyāyikas and Mīmāṁsakas.

The Buddhist logicians like Diṅnāga and Dharmakīrti reject the scepticism aired by the Cārvākas and maintain that a general statement relating two things or events should be admitted to be true, when it is based on a universally accepted principle and made ground for everyday activity (Hiriyanna 1994: 200). They refer to the maxim that doubt is limited until it leads to self-contradiction or absurdity in practical absurdity (*vyāghātāvadhirāśaṅkā*). However, the Buddhists are keen to limit invariable concomitance to cases wherein the relationship is logically demonstrable. Accordingly, they maintain that two objects are invariably related only when they are having the relationship of identity (*tādātmya*) as in the case of copper and metal or causality (*tadutpatti*) as in the case of smoke and fire. To illustrate, one can infer that if the given thing is copper, it is also a metal, on the basis of the relationship of identity. Similarly, one can infer fire from smoke on the basis of causality, as smoke is caused by fire. The Buddhists do not accept any other relation between the *probans* and the *probandum*. For example, they do not accept inference, as in the case of the presence of horns in an animal which has cloven hoofs. The reason is that there is no satisfactory explanation to the question as to "Why should cloven hoofs be associated with horns?".

The Naiyāyikas, on the other hand, are not unduly worried about the strictures of the Cārvākas against inference. Inference, in fact, happens to be their staple diet, the means of valid knowledge par excellence and they are not prepared to abandon or modify their key concept in any manner against the scepticism. Nor do they, like the Buddhists, believe in narrowing the scope of invariable concomitance just to overcome the Cārvāka objection.

They do not admit the position that inference concerns the *probans* and the *probandum* in their universal aspect. Inference is always from particular to particular. We infer the presence of a particular fire from the perception of a particular smoke. It is obvious from this that there is no question of establishing something already established (*siddhasādhanam*), as alleged by the Cārvākas, since one does not previously know the presence of a particular fire in a particular substratum before the inference. The Naiyāyikas postulate a suprasensory (*alaukika*) type of perception to explain the deductive process through which the invariable relation is arrived at (Sastri 1932: 206). Thus when one comes to have visual perception of smoke and fire, all particular smokes and fires are brought under its purview through the contact called generic (*sāmānya lakṣaṇā*). Accordingly, the relationship assumed between the perceived smoke and fire is extended to instances of smoke and fire not directly perceived (*Kārikāvalī* I.65). The Naiyāyikas further plug loopholes in faulty reasoning through their meticulously conceived concept of faulty reason (*hetvābhāsa*), which, like the notion of fallacy in Western logic, results in wrong conclusion.

The Naiyāyikas do not believe that one is by nature sceptical of the validity of the invariable concomitance. Viśvanātha Pañcānana avers that it is not even necessary for one to have repeated experience of the co-presence of the *probans* and *probandum* like smoke and fire; a single perception will be sufficient to arrive at their relatedness provided that there is no doubt about their invariability.[1] Sometimes, when a doubt arises, it can be removed through repeated observation. When even repeated observation fails, the doubt can be removed by counterargument (*tarka*). Thus, if a doubt arises that there could be smoke even in places devoid of fire, it can be warded off with the counterargument: If this substratum were not having fire, it would not have smoke either, as without a cause, there cannot be an effect. If, further, doubt persists that there could be effect without cause, the principle of

[1] *bhūyodaśanam tu na kāraṇam vyabhicārasphūrtau sakṛddarśane 'pi kvacid vyāptigrahāt* I – *Kārikāvalī*, p. 454

inconsistency (*vyāghāta*) may be evoked to remove such doubts. In other words, if it were argued that there could be effect without cause, it would incur the admission that one could get smoke without fire or attain the feeling of satisfaction without eating food. Viśvanātha hastens to add that if there is no doubt at all, there is no requirement of this type of counterargument.[2] According to the *Tarkasaṁgraha*, counterargument (*tarka*) is a mode of unreal experience (*ayathārthānubhava*), along with doubt (*saṁśaya*) and false knowledge (*viparyaya*). It defines counterargument as the superimposition of the pervader through the superimposition of the pervaded. The example given is: "If there were no fire, there would not be smoke." It can be seen that the whole structure of the counterargument is like an unlikely condition as in the given instance, there are both fire and smoke. The reason for including it under the category of unreal experience is that the argument projects an unreal situation. Kuppuswami Sastri glosses *tarka* as indirect argument and equates it with *reductio ad absurdum* (1932: 251). It has a variegated history in Indian philosophical tradition. In the *Nyāyasūtra* of Gautama, it appears as a category (*padārtha*) along with other cognitive forms like doubt. Vātsyāyana, in his *Bhāṣya*, maintains that it is not included in the means of valid knowledge. It is not just another means of knowledge, but it is helpful for other means of knowledge and in that sense, it is conducive to the philosophical knowledge.[3]

The Prābhākaras seem to be not unduly worried by the problem of novelty of the knowledge content in inference posed by the Cārvākas as novelty is not insisted upon as a precondition of the validity of any knowledge by them. In their view, if any normal inference like that of fire from smoke is proven to be an experience (*anubhava*) and not mere recollection (*smṛti*), it can be regarded as a valid knowledge. An inference even if it is a

---

[2] *yatra svata eva śaṅkā nāvatarati, tatra na tarkāpekṣāpīti* – *Kārikāvalī*, pp. 454-55

[3] *tarko na pramāṇasangṛhītaḥ, na pramāṇātaram, pramāṇānāmanugrāhaka statvajnānāya kalpate nyāyadṛśā* – *Nyāyadarśana*, p. 7

re-experience (*gṛhītagrāhī anubhavaḥ*) is a valid experience. The Prābhākaras also argue that invariable concomitance assumes the form of universal generalization, but they do not accept the view of the Naiyāyikas that all particulars are brought under its ambit through a suprasensory perception. They overcome the problem of particulars by maintaining that the elements of time and space do not enter into the scheme of relation represented by the invariable concomitance (Sastri 1932: 213-14).

The Bhāṭṭas, who insist on novelty as a precondition of any valid knowledge, cannot accept the position of the Prābhākaras. They try to overrule the objections of the Cārvākas elaborating the concept of counterargument (*tarka*) in their defence of invariable concomitance. Thus, Cidānanda and following him, Nārāyaṇa Bhaṭṭa, incorporate counterargument as an essential factor in arriving at invariable concomitance. According to him, one can arrive at an infallible invariable concomitance only after ascertaining that the *probandum* does not require, apart from the presence of the *probans*, the additional presence of any adventitious condition (*upādhi*) for it being established. According to Cidānanda, mere repeated observation of the co-presence of the *probans* and the *probandum* will not suffice to arrive at invariable concomitance. We can go on seeing fire and smoke together in as many instances as possible; yet their invariable concomitance may not be foolproof. The example adduced is that of the eighth child of Maitrī. Her seven children are dark and she is expecting an eighth child. Now, suppose one makes an inference that the eighth child also will be dark in colour, the inference may prove to be wrong if the darkness of the children is caused by some adventitious condition like her diet. To make invariable concomitance foolproof, counterargument also is recognized there as conducive to the valid knowledge.

In this context, Nārāyaṇa gives a succinct definition of counterargument. Three features are underlined in this definition:

1. A counterargument is resorted to when doubt occurs as to the validity of an object that it is otherwise.

2. The counterargument is adduced to refute the alternate possibility enshrined in the doubt.
3. The counterargument consists of the elucidation of the defect in the alternate position.

To illustrate, let us take the example of the inference, "this hill has fire as it has smoke", based on the assumption that whichever has smoke has fire. Here it can be doubted if smoke could be also present in places which do not have fire. Here the counterargument is that if there is no fire, there cannot be any smoke also as there cannot be any effect without a proper cause. Nārāyaṇa points out that the counterargument is called the "occasioning of the undesirable" (*aniṣṭaprasaṅga*) by the logicians.

According to the Bhāṭṭas, a counterargument has five limbs. They are:

1. Pervasion (*vyāpti*) between the assumed *probandum* and the *probans.*
2. Lack of cancellation by another counterargument (*tarkāpratihati*).
3. Finality in opposition (*viparyaye avasāna*), i.e. the assumption of something opposite to the basic premise.
4. Undesirability (*aniṣṭatva*).
5. Non-favourableness (*ananukūlatva*).

Nārāyaṇa demonstrates how all these conditions are fulfilled in the case of a typical counterargument. Accordingly, what is done by counterargument is showing the undesirable implications when accepting the position that the fact contrary to that which is taken up as valid knowledge. Thus, when one proves through inference the presence of fire in the hill on the basis of the presence of smoke, the acceptance of the absence of fire would entail the acceptance of the absence of smoke also, which goes against experience. The inference of fire can be defended only if it is possible to find an invariable concomitance between the assumed absence of fire and the absence of smoke. Then it is possible to defend the proposition against any further counterarguments adduced by the opponent. The undesirability of the implication, i.e. the absence of smoke is well known. Finally, the counterargument should also not contribute in any way to the establishment of the opposing view.

Any defect in the above-mentioned five conditions will result in the counterargument also becoming fallacious. For example, one cannot frame the following counterargument: "If there be no fire, there will not be mountainness". This is because of the fact that there is no invariable concomitance between fire and mountainness. The following counterargument is defective as it is cancelled by another: "If this cloud rise is not accompanied by rain, then it will also be not dense". This counterargument can be neutralized by another: "If it is accompanied by rain, it will not be accompanied by strong wind". In other words, the presence of strong winds has to be accounted for before determining if a particular cloud is going to make rain. The example for finality in opposition is the inference, "Sound is non-eternal, because it is produced". The counterargument is, "If the sound is not non-eternal, then it will not be produced". Actually, this opposite view is acceptable to the Bhāṭṭa Mīmāṁsakas who accept the non-production of sound, and from their standpoint, the counterargument loses all its force. The example for lack of undesirability is the same inference. Finally, the example for the lack of favourableness is action is to be inferred, since it is action, like the action of the sun. Here the counterargument is that if action were not inferred, action itself could not be established". This would be favourable to people who believe that action is an object of perception. They can establish the perceptibility of action and say that otherwise action cannot be established.

Nārāyaṇa maintains that the counterargument is useful in two places, first, at the time of the cognition of invariable concomitance, and second, at the time of the inference. In both these places, it removes any doubt regarding the variableness of the invariable concomitance and thus is conducive to the process of inference (Narāyaṇa Bhaṭṭa 1933: 39). He contends that the very presence of the counterargument is a guarantee against the epistemological scepticism of the Cārvākas that the possibility of adventitious conditions is difficult to be removed in inference. In this connection, he poses two alternatives for the Cārvāka objection: (a) Is the adventitious condition capable of being known? (b) Or is it incapable of being known? If it is incapable, it cannot be a matter of doubt at all. If it is capable of being known, the question arises as to why such an adventitious condition is not experienced. If it were an object of inference, the question arises as to why the *probans* of it is not seen. In other words, the very possibility of adventitious conditions in valid inferences can be demonstrated as a myth (ibid.: 41).

Apart from this function in inference, counterargument is actually elevated to the position of an aid of all types of means of valid knowledge in Bhāṭṭa Mīmāṁsā. Thus, according to Nārāyaṇa,

> Until there is the extermination of doubts, a series of counterarguments must be applied in all inferences. And this is saying very little; because even all means of valid knowledge, like perception and authority, cannot live without counterarguments. …
>
> – Ibid.: 42; tr. Kunhan Raja and S.S. Surya Narayana Sastri

To illustrate, the perception, "This is a jar" can have as its object the pot in its wholeness as distinguished from mere atoms which is the position of the Buddhists. This is accomplished by the counterargument: "If indeed the object were the atoms, there would not have been a unitary appearance having a magnitude."

The counterargument is also helpful in the case of verbal testimony. Thus, there is a prescription in Veda that one should study one's own Veda (*svādhyāyo 'dhyetavyaḥ*). Here it is the principle of prolixity (*gaurava*) with the aid of which the counterargument settles the doubt about the result of teaching. Now there can be a doubt about the fruit of this prescription: whether the purpose of the prescription is attainment of the heaven or comprehension of the meaning of the scripture. Here the counterargument is that when one postulates an unseen thing (attainment of heaven) as the fruit when there is a seen one (the comprehension of meaning), it entails prolixity. This argument settles the issue and helps one reach the conclusion that the fruit is the comprehension of the meaning. The opposite counterargument, "If the fruit be to know the meaning, then the prescription will be in vain", has to be rejected whenever it arises, in view of this.

Another instance is the prescription in the *Manusmr̥ti* that a twice born who would teach the Veda to his disciple along with *kalpa* and mysteries after initiating him is called the preceptor. Here doubt may occur as to the import of this prescription: Does it prescribe teaching or preceptorhood? Here the counterargument is this: If it were a mere prescription of teaching, the sentence will have no unity of structure as it will leave out the portion "he is called a preceptor". This would conclusively prove that the import of the prescription is in assigning preceptorhood to the teacher. Yet another example of verbal cognition being aided by counterargument is related to the prescription "one shall bring near the smeared stones (*āktāḥ śarkarāḥ uapadadhāti*)". Here doubt may arise if the smearing is to be done with ghee or oil or any other substance (Narayaṇa Bhaṭṭa 1933: 316 fn). And it is removed with the counterargument that if it is done without ghee, there will be conflict with the rest of the sentence, *tejo vai ghr̥tam* (verily, ghee is fire). Thus, demonstrating that investigation in the form of counterargument is an aid in the establishment of all meanings of sentences, Nārāyaṇa quotes Manu:

> And he who establishes the utterances of sages and moral instructions through counterarguments not conflicting with the scriptural science knows the *dharma* and none else.
>
> – *Manusmr̥ti* XVII.106

To conclude, it can be seen that philosophers of all hues in India have taken up the challenge of the opponents quite seriously regarding the validity and worth of inference in promoting the understanding of the objective world. Science and technology progresses on the basis of the premise that the phenomena can be explained and predicted with the help of universal laws which, in their turn, seem to be based on the principle of the regularity and orderliness of the universe. Even social sciences base their methodology on the assumption of the validity of broad generalizations. Repeated observations through experimentations and fieldwork are universally accepted as valid methods of enhancing our awareness of the physical universe and the social relations of mankind. To deny all this will be opening up the Pandora's Box of unlimited scepticism and it is difficult to believe if the Cārvākas ever subscribed to such a world view. The Buddhist remedy of delimiting the scope of invariable concomitance only to demonstrable areas of causality and identity also results in denying vast areas of inferable and very useful deductive information from the arena of valid knowledge. It is in this context that the notion of counterargument acquires tremendous significance. It is actually *reductio ad absurdum*, as its methodology consisting in exposing the vulnerability of the opponent's position. Nārāyaṇa and others have demonstrated that this mode of reasoning helps one not only to defend valid cases of inference, but also to detect the import of other means of valid knowledge.

3

Inference as a Means of Valid Knowledge in Indian Epistemological Tradition

INFERENCE (*anumāna*) is data-based knowledge by means of which one can arrive at a multitude of knowledge which is not, strictly speaking, directly accessible, but which, added to one's arsenal, makes vital contribution to the knowledge base with which one negotiates with the outside world. It is not, therefore, surprising that most of the systems of Indian philosophy accept inference as a means of valid knowledge (*pramāṇa*). There are elaborate discussions about the nature and structure of the process of inference in various orthodox and heterodox systems of Indian philosophy, but the most outstanding contributions are those of the Naiyāyikas and the Buddhists. It seems, from all this deep and mostly hair-splitting analysis, that the Indian mind had perfected the art of logical reasoning with a vigorous methodology, which probably strengthened the scientific climate of ancient India itself. Unfortunately one of the grey spots in the Indian intellectual tradition is the relative lack of methodological discussions in the otherwise impressive scientific treatises, but it is evident that most of the results arrived at in various spheres of knowledge systems like astronomy, mathematics, engineering, metallurgy, medicine, jurisprudence, aesthetics and Yoga were all based on genuine scientific approach in which inductive and deductive approaches were profusely followed. The methodological discussions, which can be gleaned from the available scientific treatises, however sparse they are, also strengthen this hypothesis. To cite an example, both Manu (XII.105-06) and Yājñavalkya (I.3), who were the prominent orthodox law givers of ancient India, recognize the importance of logical reasoning (*tarka*) in the comprehension of duty (*dharma*) from the Vedas and Kauṭilya, the statesman-cum-political philosopher, gives an honoured place to the science of reasoning in his curriculum. It seems from all this that an analysis of the perceptions on inference scattered in various philosophical treatises will be a good beginning in a multi-pronged attempt to comprehend the rich epistemological tradition of ancient India.

Inference is the deductive knowledge generated from direct experience. A typical example is the statement "This hill has fire as it has smoke" in which we infer the presence of fire in the hill on the basis of the presence of smoke therein. This inference is prompted by the knowledge of the invariable concomitance (*vyāpti*), between fire and smoke, as "wherever there is smoke, there is fire". The invariable concomitance involves both inductive and deductive reasoning. The inductive element is in the generalization from known particulars to reach a universal principle. When the generalization is applied in a particular instance to warrant a definite conclusion, as when one infers fire on the basis of the perception of smoke, it is the deductive element which is manifested. The nature and content of inference vary from system to system in Indian philosophy, and there are interesting points of debate about the syllogistic structure, nature of invariable concomitance, fallacies and nature of the inferred knowledge. Elaborate strategies are evolved in different systems to plug the possible loopholes in the inferential process so as to make inference foolproof. The present paper proposes to critically analyse the evolution of the concept of inference in various systems of Indian philosophy like Buddhism, Jainism, Nyāya–Vaiśeṣika, Mīmāṁsā and Vedānta from historical and comparative perspectives.

Though it is possible to find stray thoughts related to inference and related epistemological issues in early Vedic literature, it is during the early post-Vedic period that attitudes and perspectives crystallized into concrete epistemological thought. The impetus for this development evidently came from heterodox systems of thought like materialism, Buddhism and Jainism which staunchly opposed the Vedic authority with all the arsenal available in their armory, as a result of which adherents of Vedic tradition were forced to seek their own methods of defence. Thus there were concerted attempts in orthodox camps to address such issues like the sources of valid knowledge and the means of verifying the validity of knowledge itself. The heterodox systems also spiritedly joined the ensuing debates. It is thus Indian philosophy became self-conscious and adapted methods to defend the foundational tenets of its systems. Most of the systems accepted inference as a means of valid knowledge even though their concept of inference including its nature and structure differed substantially.

The term *anumāna* literally means "after proof" and the term signifies knowledge derived from other types of knowledge, mainly perception and in schools following scriptural authority, verbal testimony. Among the various schools, it is the Nyāya system of logic which give prominence to inference in a marked way, though the contribution of Buddhist schools is also substantial. The importance given by logicians of the Nyāya-fold can be gauged from the statement that they were fond of substantiating the validity of even objects directly perceived. The Nyāya system was initially known as also Ānvīkṣikī and Vātsyāyana, the author of *Nyāyasūtrabhāṣya*, glosses the term *anvīkṣā* as *anumāna*, maintaining that the chief main of Nyāya is to elucidate *anvīkṣā* as a means of valid knowledge.

According to the Naiyāyikas, and also Buddhists, inference is twofold: that which is for one's sake (*svārthānumāna*) and that which is for the sake of others (*parārthānumāna*). The former is quite internal and does not require linguistic form at all. The latter is to persuade the listener to follow the logical steps in the inference of the given example, and hence necessarily couched in language. From this classification, it is evident that the linguistic form which is associated with inference in its syllogistic form is not an essential constituent of its structure. As pointed out by Hiriyanna, it is a rejection of the common Western verbal notion of logic (1994: 255). It is generally accepted that while Western logic emphasizes the formal accept of the syllogism, Indian logicians were more concerned with its material aspect. The Italian philosopher Benedetto Croce brings out the importance of the distinction between *svārthānumāna* and *parārthānumāna* thus:

> Indian Logic studies the naturalistic syllogism in *itself* as internal thought, distinguishing it from the syllogism *for others*, that is to say, from the more or less usual, but always extrinsic and always accidental form of communication and dispute. It has not even a suspicion of the extravagant idea (which still vitiates our treatises) of a truth which is merely syllogistic and formalist, and which may be false in fact. It takes no account of the judgement, or rather it considers what is called judgement and what is really the proposition as verbal clothing of language: it does not make the verbal distinctions of subject, copula and predicate; it does not admit classes of categorical and hypothetical, of affirmative and of negative judgements. All these are extraneous to Logic, whose subject is the constant: knowledge considered in itself.
>
> – Qtd. Hiriyanna 1994: 256

The syllogism of the Naiyāyikas is called "five-membered sentence" (*pañcāvayava-vākya*) and a typical instance of inferring fire from smoke in the hill has the following five steps:

1. This mountain has fire.
2. For it has smoke.
3. Whatever has smoke has fire, e.g. the kitchen.
4. This mountain has smoke which is invariably accompanied by fire.
5. Therefore this mountain has fire.

The Buddhists and the Mīmāṁsakas do not accept all these five steps. The Mīmāṁsakas stick to a three-membered syllogism, arguing that either the first three or the last three alone are necessary. According to the Buddhists, the third and the fourth steps alone are sufficient (Sastri 1932: 227). It can be seen that the first item and the last one are repetitions, but the Naiyāyikas argue that these are necessary steps in the formal process of inference to ensure that the *probans* consisting of smoke perceived by the person who makes the inference is qualified by the invariable concomitance that wherever there is smoke, there is fire. It is a formal synthesis of the major premise mentioned in the third sentence and the minor premise of the first sentence. This elaborated syllogism can be contrasted with the simpler Aristotelian syllogism which runs as follows:

All men are mortal
Socrates is a man
Therefore Socrates is mortal.

Here, it is the middle term which implicitly links the major and minor premises. On the other hand, in the Nyāya model, all the three terms are interlinked in the subsumptive reflection. The inductive-cum-deductive nature of the process of inference is evident from the general rule accompanied by the example (Hiriyanna 1994: 257). It may be worth mentioning in this context that early Naiyāyikas restricted the inferential process to the sensuous sphere, and believed that reasoning is from particulars to particulars, and it was probably Diṅnāga, the Buddhist logician, who propounded the view that it is through the universal that the particular proceeds to particular (ibid.).

The key concept of the inferential process is *vyāpti* (invariable concomitance) which is expressed through the form "wherever there is smoke, there is fire", on the basis of which one successfully infers the presence of fire in the hill due to the perceived presence of smoke. *Vyāpti* literally means pervasion and it is the universal nature of the relation which is hinted at by the term as it implies that the rule holds good anywhere, anytime. According to the Naiyāyikas, we arrive at the cognition of this relation between frequent sight of both the smoke and fire in known instances. If we are to believe the representations in rival treatises, the

Cārvākas did not accept inference as a means of valid knowledge as they suspected that invariable concomitance rests on very flimsy grounds. According to them, there is no sufficient ground to believe in the truth of the universal relation arrived through inductive reasoning (ibid.: 189). Even if it is conceded that observation of known facts warrants the assumption of invariable relation between, say smoke and fire, the Cārvākas contend that there is no guarantee that it will hold good in uninvestigated and unknown cases also. If it is argued that the relation is confined to essential features of universals unrelated to particulars, then inference will cease to be of any practical relevance as particulars are left out. The Cārvākas argue further that our belief in the validity of inference is only a psychological process and no logical certitude can be attached to it. This would explain the difference among rational philosophers themselves concerning even essential matters (ibid.: 190). One big loophole of this ingenious reasoning is that it itself, being arrived at through induction, validates the proposition it wishes to refute, that *vyāpti* is not valid.

The Mīmāṁsakas of the Bhāṭṭa school meet this objection with the argument that inference is really from particulars to particulars and any appearance on the contrary could be explained away. The Naiyāyikas postulate a suprasensory (*alaukika*) type of perception to explain the deductive process through which the invariable relation is arrived at (Sastri 1932: 206). Thus when one comes to have visual perception of smoke and fire, all particular smokes and fires are brought under its purview through the contact called generic (*sāmānya lakṣaṇā*). Accordingly, the relationship assumed between the perceived smoke and fire is extended to instances of smoke and fire not directly perceived (*Siddhāntamuktāvalī* I.65). On the other hand, Buddhist logicians like Diṅnāga and Dharmakīrti conceive of the relation in a negative way insisting that the *probans* should not exist in the absence of the *probandum* and describe the relation as invariableness (*avinābhāva*) (Sastri 1932: 207). They reject the scepticism aired by the Cārvākas and maintain that a general statement relating two things or events should be admitted to be true, when it is based on a universally accepted principle and made ground for everyday activity (Hiriyanna 1994: 200). They refer to the maxim that doubt is limited until it leads to self-contradiction or absurdity in practical absurdity (*vyāghātāvadhirāśaṅkā*). However, the Buddhists are keen to limit invariable concomitance to cases wherein the relationship is logically demonstrable. Accordingly, they maintain that two objects are invariably related only when they are having the relationship of identity (*tādātmya*) as in the case of copper and metal or causality (*tadutpatti*) as in the case of smoke and fire. To illustrate, one can infer that if the given thing is copper, it is also a metal, on the basis of the relationship of identity. Similarly, one can infer fire from smoke on the basis of causality, as smoke is caused by fire. The insistence on either of these relations means that the Buddhists do not consider the inference of one object from another, even if they are, for all practical purposes, concomitant, as in the case of the presence of horns in an animal which has cloven hoofs.

The Naiyāyikas further plug loopholes in faulty reasoning through their meticulously conceived concept of faulty reason, (*hetvābhāsa*) which, like the Western notion of fallacy, results in wrong conclusion. The main difference between *hetvābhāsa* and fallacy is that while the former is used in the sense of a defective conclusion or interpretation resulting from a defective process of thinking, the latter is a defective reason. The term *hetvābhāsa* literally means a "semblance of reason" and in it, usually the defective *probans* appears very much similar to a valid *probans*. The five fallacious *probans* accepted by the Naiyāyikas are the following:

1. *Variable* (*savyabhicāra*): Here the *probans* is not conclusive as it is not invariably related to the *probandum*. It is further classified into three, viz. common (*sādhāraṇa*), uncommon (*asādhāraṇa)* and inconclusive (*anupasaṁhārin*).

   a. *Common*: Here the *probans* is common to instances of examples and counterexamples alike and hence not capable of proving the *probandum*. Example: "This mountain has fire, as it is knowable". Here knowability is common to a lake also, which has no fire.

b. *Uncommon*: Here the *probans* exists only in the subject and not anywhere else and hence is not convincing. Example: "Fire is hot, as it is fire". Here fireness, the *probans* is found only in the subject (*pakṣa*), and neither in similar example (*udāharaṇa*) nor in counterexample (*vipakṣa*).

c. *Inconclusive*. Here the *probans* has neither positive nor negative examples. Example "All things are transient, since they are knowable". Here there is no example available to demonstrate the invariable concomitance as all objects fall within the purview of the subject (*pakṣa*).

2. The adverse reason (*viruddha*). Here the *probans* is invariably concomitant with the very absence of the *probandum*. Example: "The road is dry as it has been raining".

3. The opposable reason (*satpratipakṣa*). Here the *probans* can be countered by an equally patent fact which proves just the contrary. Example: "This man is healthy since he is fat". Here the contrary can be proven with another fact like his age.

4. The unestablished reason (*asiddha*) has an unestablished aspect about it. It is divided into three: Having unestablished substratum (*āśrayāsiddha*), unestablished in itself (*svarūpāsiddha*) and unestablished in respect of its concomitance (*vyāpyatvāsiddha*).

   a. *The reason with unestablished substratum*: Example: "Sky-lotus is fragrant, since it is a lotus, like a lotus in the lake". Here we cannot establish the existence of an entity called sky lotus and the proposition hence becomes faulty.

   b. *Reason unestablished in itself*: "Cotton is heavy since it is a metal". Here the quality of being a metal does not exist in the subject and hence the reason is defective.

   c. *Unestablished in respect of its concomitance*: Here the *probans* is accompanied by an adventitious condition

> (*upādhi*) which is pervasive with the *probandum*. In other words, the *probans* requires the condition that it is accompanied by another agent to ensure the presence of the *probandum*. An example would be "This mountain has smoke since it has fire". Now, fire itself does not guarantee the presence of smoke. It requires the presence of the adventitious condition of contact with wet fuel (*ārdrendhana saṁyoga*) for proving the presence of smoke.

To conclude, it can be seen that Indian logicians had perfected the concept of inference plugging all loopholes for faulty reasoning and making it a tool for argumentation and substantiation. We do not know how far the methodology followed in the philosophical texts was followed in empirical sciences, but the fund of knowledge available must have definitely enriched the armoury of scientists of all hues. As pointed out earlier, we see glimpses of the logical process envisaged in treatises related to jurisprudence, astronomy, medicine and some other systems of knowledge and these should be probed into to reconstruct the intellectual history of India.

4

The Impact of Navya-Nyāya on Sanskrit Poetics with Special Reference to Jagannātha Paṇḍita

NAVYA-NYĀYA, which emerged as a distinct school of thought with the advent of Gaṅgeśopādhyāya's *Nyāyatattvacintāmaṇi*, has ushered in great change in Indian philosophical thinking (Sastri 1932: xxxv-xxxvii). Indian logic arms itself with the most sophisticated tools of linguistic analysis in this seminal work. The earlier ontological orientation of the Nyāya system is here replaced by a vigorous epistemological predilection which is even outwardly manifested in the nomenclature adapted for each section of the work: chapters are here arranged under the four means of valid knowledge consisting of perception, inference, analogy and verbal testimony in the place of ontological categories like substance and quality. It is, however, in the subtlety of analysis that Navya-Nyāya stands apart from sister disciplines. This feat was achieved by the protagonists of the school by developing ingenious tools with which they could disambiguate language and create a thoroughly precise mode of representation of logical structures inherent in thought processes. The success achieved by the Navya-Naiyāyikas in this respect was so decisive that other systems of thought had little choice save the adaptation of the techniques of the former in their own works. Even systems like Vedānta which give more importance to scripture than to logic are no exception to this general tendency. The present paper is an attempt to investigate the nature of changes brought about in discourses related to poetics caused by the interface of the discipline with Navya-Nyāya logic, as exemplified in the *Rasagaṅgādhara*, the magnum opus of Jagannātha Paṇḍit, which represents a paradigmatic shift in the discourse in tone and tenor, in probably the most serious and thoroughgoing exercise to make poetics a *śāstra*.

It should be acknowledged at the very outset that the greatness of the *Rasagaṅgādhara* owes as much to the originality and free thinking of the author as to the neatness with which he has represented his arguments using the terminology of Navya-Nyāya. It is also a fact that Jagannātha seldom subscribes to the ontology and epistemology of Navya-Nyāya when it comes to the basics, wherein he has a strong Vedāntic leaning.[1] But this does not prevent him from using the concepts and terminology of Navya-Nyāya, rather in an eclitical fashion, to present his arguments and to refute the views of his opponents.

The fundamental theoretical changes brought about in poetics by Jagannātha Paṇḍit may be summarized at the outset before we proceed to examine the impact of Navya-Nyāya logic on his mode of arguments. Jagannātha, contrary to the generally held view that word and sense constitute poetry, avers that it is only the word of course representing beautiful meaning which constitutes poetry. With regard to the causes of poetry, while the majority of poeticians take the stand that the intuitive genius, erudition and constant exercise combinedly are responsible for it, Jagannātha maintains that poetry is caused by *pratibhā*, which he defines as the knowledge of word and sense which are conducive for the composition of poetry and this, in turn, is caused either by unseen merit or the combination of erudition and exercise. With regard to the threefold division of poetry, as superior, mediocre and inferior, attempted by poeticians like Mammaṭa, he avers that it does not do justice to *guṇībhūtavyaṅgya* and *arthacitra* and, therefore, proposes a fourfold classification, incorporating "the very best" (*uttamottama*) and promoting *dhvani*, *guṇībhūtavyaṅgya*

[1] See, for his "Navya" theory of *rasa* wherein he subscribes to the view of Vedānta that *rasa* is the result of an illusion.

and *arthacitra* to the *uttamottama*, *uttama* and *madhyama* varieties (*Rasagaṅgādhara*, p. 24). Severely criticizing Appaya Dīkṣita for demonstrating that the suggested sense is invariably related to the expressed sense, he makes it clear that such a hermeneutical position would be more in tune with Mahima Bhaṭṭa's argument that the so-called suggested sense is inferred. Jagannātha offers clarification to Abhinavagupta's interpretation of *rasasūtra* and maintains that it is the inherent consciousness characterized by the basic mental state, rather than the basic mental state characterized by the consciousness, which constitutes the *rasa*. He mentions eleven interpretations of the *rasasūtra* among which a couple is evidently the handiwork of his own. He criticizes the view of Mammaṭa that *guṇa*s are qualities of *rasa* since *rasa* being the soul has no qualities (Ramachandrudu 1983: 163). Another important contribution of Jagannātha is his contention that in homonymous words, the non-contextual meaning is also got through the process of denotation (*abhidhā*) and it is the figure involved that is suggested. He also elaborates the process of verbal cognition in varieties of *upamā* using the tools of *śābdabodha* developed in works like the *Vyutpattivāda*. He further makes subtler principles of distinction of various figures like *upamā*.

II

Let us now explore how far the techniques of Navya-Nyāya help Jagannātha to build his formidable citadels of arguments in defence of his positions. First, he demolishes the view of opponents that poetry is constituted by word and meaning, which has been repeated verbatim from earlier poeticians onwards without any critical examination. Jagannātha has a simple question to ask: What is the basis of the contention that *both* word and meaning constitute poetry? The view of the opponent itself cannot be taken as a proof, since it begs the question. On the other hand, we have usages like "poetry is recited aloud", "poetry is heard, sense not understood", and "sense is understood from poetry" which evidently bifurcate sense from poetry. Jagannātha anticipates the argument that such expressions can be explained as metaphorical liberties of usage, but to concede that position, he reminds his opponents that they should cite some examples wherein the word poetry is used in the sense of both word and sense. Further, he introduces the concepts of partial existence (*vyāsajyavṛtti*) and separate existence (*pratyekaparyāpta*) to demolish the theory. If the quality of being poetry were partially existing in both the word and the sense, neither of them by itself could be referred to as poetry, since the other element also will be required to give the status of poetry to either word or sense. This would lead one to argue that usages like "a sentence of verse is not poetry" which are patently wrong are valid. On his part, Jagannātha sticks to the position that it is word which describes meaning giving rise to cognition generating super mundane pleasure which constitutes poetry. He cordons off unpoetic utterances from the purview of poetry by

1. introducing the concept of aesthetic contemplation (*bhāvanā*), which is aesthetics specific in the place of cognition (*jñāna*) which is of a more generic nature to ward off "cognitive jumbles" (*samuhālambana jñāna*).
2. introducing an elaborate definition as "that the aesthetic contemplation of the meaning described by which generates aesthetic delight (*camatkāra*)" to ward off sentence cognitions figuring in succession of cognitions (*dhārāvāhika-jñāna*).
3. yet again improvising the definition by directly connecting aesthetic delight to the word through the relation of the revealer of meaning which possesses the state of being the generator of aesthetic delight (*svaviśiṣṭajanakatāvacchedakārthapradipādakatāsaṁsargeṇa camatkāratvavatvam*). In poetry, the word describes meaning, which generates aesthetic delight. This definition is to avoid the cumbersome employment of "that" and "which" (*yacchabda* and *tacchabda*).

All this ingenuity results in a foolproof definition of poetry. The sea change brought about in the definition is indicative of the quantum leap achieved by Jagannātha Paṇḍit in dialectics. He also refutes the contention of Mammaṭa and others that the word and sense should be devoid of defects to be called poetry pointing out that in that case, one cannot account for usages like "defective poetry" (*Rasagaṅgādhara*, p. 8).

With regard to the causes of poetry, Jagannātha effects a radical change in the very notion of *pratibhā* by converting it from an intuitive talent to mere competence in word and sense conducive to the composition of poetry. What he has done is creating a casual chain with poetry at the extreme end, caused by *pratibhā* which in its turn is caused either by unseen merit (*adṛṣṭa*) or the combination of erudition (*vyutpatti*) and exertion (*abhyāsa*). Thus he transfers the uncertainty principle behind it – it is well known that only some people possess it – to the unseen (*adṛṣṭa*) merit and maintains that *pratibhā* is of different nature based on its causes. He counters the argument of the opponent that such notion of parallel cause–effect chain will result in mutual cancellation. The *pratibhā* caused by unseen merit is qualitatively different from that caused by erudition and exertion and vice versa and hence each does not substitute the other. To the query as to why there is no *pratibhā* despite erudition and exertion, he answers that the cause in such instances is not characterized by the necessary delimiting adjunct (*avacchedaka*), or in simple terms, there is no sufficient erudition and exertion to warrant the genesis of poetry. He further discusses the problem whether *pratibhātva* is a generic attribute (*jāti*) or an adventitious quality (*upādhi*). Though he does not have any objection to its being a generic attribute, he says that it could be taken as an undifferentiated adventitious adjunct (*akhaṇḍopādhi*) like *ākāśatva* rather than a differentiated adjunct (*sakhaṇḍopādhi*) like *nīlaghaṭatva*. This is tantamount to the admission that the delimiting adjunct of poetic genius is uniform and unique and it does not have any adjective.

Jagannātha makes use of Navya-Nyāya tools in describing the functions of language (*śabda-vyāpāra*), like *abhidhā* and *lakṣaṇā*. However, he does not subscribe to the view of the Naiyāyikas that the denotative power of a word (*abhidhā*) exists in the individual characterized by generic attribute. Probably due to his Vedānta orientation, which accepts the Mīmāṁsaka epistemology at the practical level, he follows the Mīmāṁsaka view that the denotative power exists in the generic attribute like cowness and that the individual, like the cow, is known through inevitable presumption (*ākṣepa*) (*Rasagaṅgādhara*, p. 182). He rejects the contention of the Vaiyākaraṇas also that the denotative power of words exists in the generic attribute (*jāti*), qualities (*guṇa*), action (*kriyā*) and accidental features (*yadṛcchā*) since it involves the postulation of an extrasensory perception (*alaukika pratyakṣa*) of all the individuals not coming under the direct perception of the individual. In the case of *lakṣaṇā*, he follows the definition Naiyāyikas as *śakyasambandha*, as seen in the *Siddhāntamuktāvalī*. Also, following Naiyāyikas, he makes incongruity of intention (*tātparyānupapatti*), rather than incongruity of the syntactical relation (*anvayānupapatti*) as the root cause of *lakṣaṇā*.

III

One of the most outstanding contributions of Jagannātha Paṇḍit to Alaṁkāraśāstra is his examination of the mode of verbal cognition (*śābdabodha*) of *upamā*. In fact, he is the first author in Sanskrit poetics to have attempted this, to be emulated by later authors like Viśveśvara Paṇḍit. Here he accommodates the views of both the Naiyāyikas who do not accept similarity (*sādṛśya*) as a category and the Mīmāṁsakas who accept it as a category. In accordance with the Mīmāṁsaka view, he proposes *śābdabodha* in a manner as illustrated below (*Rasagaṅgādhara*, pp. 246-55):

1. *aravindasundaram mukham:* Here he proposes *lakṣaṇā* in the word *aravinda* as *aravindanirūpitasādṛśyaprayojaka* and allows it to be directly construed with *sundara*, meaning *saundaryavadabhinnam* through the relationship of non-difference as per the dictum *nipātātiriktanāmārthanāmārthayoḥ abhedenānvayaḥ*. The *ekadeśānvaya* here has to be acceptable as in *devadattasya naptā.* Alternately the word *aravinda* itself can be regarded as the locus of *lakṣaṇā* and the word *sundara* can be considered as *tātparyagrāhaka.* If we

accept the Nyāya position that similarity is not a separate category, but simply the common attribute (*samāna dharma*), the expression would mean *aravindavṛttisamānadharmā-bhinnasaundaryavadabhinnam mukham*. Here *aravinda* conveys *aravindavṛttisamānadharma* through *lakṣaṇā.*

Viśveśvara Paṇḍit, however objects to the postulation of *lakṣaṇā* here at all since it is, by common consent, *vācakaluptā.*

2. In *aravindamiva sundaram,* the particle *iva* expresses similarity. *Aravinda* is related to similarity in the relation of *nirūpitatva,* i.e. as similarity with regard to then lotus. It is related to *saundarya,* a part of the word sense of *sundara* in causative relationship. The ensuing cognition will be "the face has beauty which is non-different from the causative of the similarity in relation to the lotus".
3. In *gaja iva gacchati* (He walks like an elephant), *gaja,* by *lakṣaṇā* means *gajagamana* and *gacchati* means *gamanāśrayaḥ* (the substratum of the acting of going). Accordingly, the expression means "He has the volition conducive to walking which causes similarity to the walking of an elephant" (*gaja-gamananirūpitasādṛśyaprayojakagamanānūkūlakṛtmān*).

Jagannātha makes an important clarification in the *śābdabodha* process. Normally, all the meanings of words juxtaposed are joined together in a relation of non-difference as in the expression, *nīlam utpalam,* which means *utpala* which is non-different from *nīla.* In order to get relations like *nirūpita* (with relation to), *prayojaka* (causative), etc. the relevant word should use suffixes like that of the instrumental or genitive or other case, as in *candreṇa sadṛśaḥ* (similar in relation to the moon). But when the adjunct of the qualified object (*viśeṣyatā*) is conveyed through nouns and particles, this rule will not be applicable. As a result, in expressions like *aravindamiva sundaram* the verbal cognition will become problematic. Hence, to cover such instances, he suggests the amendment that the meanings of particles (*nipāta*s) like *iva* should also be covered for *bhedānvaya* (relatedness in difference). This will also help us to explain expressions like *ghaṭo na paṭaḥ* where *paṭa* and negation are related through the relation of countercorrelative (*pratiyogitā*) and *ghaṭa* and negation related through self-relation (*svarūpasambandha*).

Jagannātha touches upon the epistemological problems related to figurative poetry in his discussion of the verbal cognition in figures like *rūpaka*. Here, in expressions like "the face is moon", according to one school, the meaning cognized is only that "the face is non-different from the object which has the qualities of moon" (*candragataguṇavadabhinnam mukham*); the notion that "the face is non-different from moon" occurs only at a later phase, through suggestion. Since suggested meaning is immune to stultification (*bādha*), it is not cancelled by our common-sense notion. But according the newer school, there is no necessity to postulate suggestion (*lakṣaṇā*) here. The identification brought out is called *āhārya* (deliberate) since we identify these objects consciously, even when we are aware of their difference, and not mistakenly, in which case, the error would have to be regarded as sublated. This brilliant perspective ingeniously frees the imaginative world of poetry from the scrutiny of compatibility with the world of reality.

It is not possible even to enumerate similar brilliant ideas seen scattered throughout in the *Rasagaṅgādhara* in a small paper like this. Suffice to sum up that through his monumental work, Jagannātha has successfully tried to instill life to the discourse of Alaṁkāraśāstra which was facing retardation of growth after the heyday of its creative period.

5

Nyāya and Other Systems of Indian Philosophy

THE Nyāya is described as logical realism and Vaiśeṣika as atomistic pluralism and both represent orthodox systems of logic and reasoning, accepting the validity of the scriptures. In Indian tradition, the Nyāya philosophy is always associated with Vaiśeṣika philosophy and often they are referred to as the Nyāya–Vaiśeṣika system. This is probably because of the fact that they converged and synthesized with each other in the later medieval period as is seen in works like the *Tarkasaṁgraha* and *Siddhāntamuktāvalī*. However, they had different origins and historical development in the initial stages. The Nyāya philosophy seems to have originated as a part of Vedic exegesis in the early post-Vedic period (Sastri 1932: ix). The term Nyāya in its original usage signified "maxim" and was used in the sense of the principles and the logical method of Mīmāṁsā philosophy, a sense which is retained even in later works like the *Mīmāṁsā-Nyāya-prakāśa*. It is significant that law givers like Manu (XII.105-06) and Yājñavalkya (I.3) stress the importance of Nyāya in the comprehension of *dharma* and evidently they had Vedic hermeneutical principle in their mind. The Vaiśeṣikas, on the other hand, were another distinct stream altogether, and they seem to have originated outside the Vedic circles, and were even hostile to the scriptural authority. According to Kuppuswami Sastri:

> Some of these doctrines perhaps shaped themselves into the

> Sāṁkhya thought of the pre-Buddhistic stage, with a marked degree of hostility to Vedic ritualism. Some other doctrine of this kind gave rise to the pre-Buddhist logic and metaphysics of the Vaiśeṣika, with a special leaning in favour of the inductive method of reasoning based on observation and analysis and with a simple rationalistic scheme of two sources of valid knowledge (perception and inference {*pratyakṣa* and *anumāna*}) – 1932: x

Later, with the advent of heterodox systems like Buddhism, the logical method of the Vedic exegetics got itself disentangled from its Vedic environment and became closer to the Vaiśeṣika reasoning, with the result that the sister schools of Nyāya and Vaiśeṣika came into existence around fourth century CE, with the former focused on the aspects of inductive reasoning and the latter mainly concerned with inductive observation and analysis. In other words, the main concern of the Nyāya was epistemology while Vaiśeṣika was more interested in ontological problems. They were never regarded as rival systems and described as "similar systems" (*samāna tantras*). This fraternal relation is the result of a tendency described as syncretism. However, around tenth century, these systems got further synthesized when works like the *Saptapadārthī* of Śivāditya were written. Later, with Gaṅgeśopādhyāya writing his *Tattvacintāmaṇi*, the Nyāya system took a linguistic turn with ingenious methods to disambiguate knowledge and to organize knowledge formally on the basis of epistemological principles.

The Nyāya system, unlike idealistic schools like Mahāyāna Buddhism and Advaita Vedānta, believe in the existence of objects beyond their knowledge. Hence it can be regarded as logical realism. The system classifies the phenomena into seven categories (*padārthas*) called substances, qualities, action, generality, specificity, inherence and non-existence. According to Viśvanātha Pañcānana, these categories were first formulated by the Vaiśeṣikas and later accepted by the Naiyāyikas also (*Siddhāntamuktāvalī* I.2). Accordingly, the system accepts the reality of the external objects revealed through knowledge. In order to account for the experience of selfhood, the system accepts self also as a category and over and above the individual selves, a supreme self who is identical with

God. The material world consists of aggregates like earth, air, water, fire, ether, time, space, soul and mind. The concrete substances of earth, air, fire and air can be further analysed until we reach the finest particle called atom which is further unanalysable and each atom, as well as the other substances which are unanalysable are characterized by individuality (*viśeṣa*). Because of this, the Nyāya–Vaiśeṣika system can be regarded as atomic pluralism to differentiate it from the Sāṁkhya dualism and Advaitic non-dualism. The system has to reject the dualism of the Sāṁkhya, the monism of Advaitins and the nihilism of certain schools of Buddhism.

Nyāya and Buddhist Schools

It is to refute the criticism levelled by heterodox systems, notably Buddhists, that the Nyāya philosophy armed itself with logic and epistemological tools. The Naiyāyikas cite the view of the Yogācāra school which denies eternal soul and postulate the flow of knowledge. According to the Yogācāras, there is neither the knower nor the known and knowledge alone is the sole reality. No external factor is responsible for the genesis of knowledge, but only the impressions of the past experiences (Hiriyanna 1994: 205). Countering this view, the Naiyāyikas ask the question if this type of knowledge covers the entire world: if so, it will entail the postulation of omniscience to the person possessing such knowledge. If, on the other hand, it is concerned with individual objects, there are no determining factors to warrant such specific knowledge; moreover, if knowledge requires no external object, one will have to postulate knowledge even in deep sleep. Nor can be a type of knowledge without any specific form postulated. Nor can it be argued that the perishable body itself is the soul, as it fails to account for the innate impressions of each individual (*Siddhāntamuktāvalī* I.41).

The Naiyāyikas share the view of the Buddhists about inference that it is twofold: that which is for one's sake (*svārthānumāna*) and that which is for the sake of others (*parārthānumāna*). The former is quite internal and does not require linguistic form at all. The latter is to persuade the listener to follow the logical steps in the inference of the given example, and hence necessarily couched in language. From this classification, it is evident that the linguistic form which is associated with inference in its syllogistic form is not an essential constituent of its structure. As pointed out by Hiriyanna, it is a rejection of the common Western verbal notion of logic (1994: 255). It is generally accepted that while Western logic emphasizes the formal acceptance of the syllogism, Indian logicians were more concerned with its material aspect.

The syllogism of the Naiyāyikas is called "five membered sentence" (*pañcāvayava-vākya*) and a typical instance of inferring fire from smoke in the hill has the following five steps:

1. This mountain has fire.
2. For it has smoke.
3. Whatever has smoke has fire, e.g. kitchen.
4. This mountain has smoke which is invariably accompanied by fire.
5. Therefore this mountain has fire.

The Buddhists and the Mīmāṁsakas do not accept all these five steps. The Mīmāṁsakas stick to a three-membered syllogism, arguing that either the first three or the last three alone are necessary. According to the Buddhists, the third and the fourth steps alone are sufficient (Sastri 1932: 227). It can be seen that the first item and the last one are repetitions, but the Naiyāyikas argue that these are necessary steps in the formal process of inference to ensure that the *probans* consisting of smoke perceived by the person who makes the inference is qualified by the invariable concomitance that wherever there is smoke, there is fire. It is a formal synthesis of the major premise mentioned in the third sentence and the minor premise of the first sentence.

Nyāya and Cārvākas

The key concept of the inferential process is *vyāpti* (invariable concomitance) which is expressed through the form "wherever there is smoke, there is fire", on the basis of which one successfully infers the presence of fire in the hill due to the perceived presence of smoke. *Vyāpti* literally means pervasion and it is the universal nature of the relation which is hinted at by the term as it implies that the rule holds good anywhere, anytime. According to the Naiyāyikas we arrive at the cognition of this relation between through frequent sight of both the smoke and fire in known instances. If we are to believe the representations in rival treatises, the Cārvākas did not accept inference as a means of valid knowledge as they suspected that invariable concomitance rests on very flimsy grounds. According to them, there is no sufficient ground to believe in the truth of the universal relation arrived through inductive reasoning (Sastri 1932: 189). Even if it is conceded that observation of known facts warrant the assumption of invariable relation between, say smoke and fire, the Cārvākas contend that there is no guarantee that it will hold good in uninvestigated and unknown cases also. If it is argued that the relation is confined to essential features of universals unrelated to particulars, then inference will cease to be of any practical relevance as particulars are left out. The Cārvākas argue further that our belief in the validity of inference is only a psychological process and no logical certitude can be attached to it. This would explain the difference among rational philosophers themselves concerning even essential matters (Sastri 1932: 190). One big loophole of this ingenious reasoning is that it itself, being arrived at through induction, validates the proposition it wishes to refute, that *vyāpti* is not valid.

The Mīmāṁsakas of the Bhāṭṭa school meet this objection with the argument that inference is really from particulars to particulars and any appearance on the contrary could be explained away. The Naiyāyikas postulate a suprasensory (*alaukika*) type of perception to explain the deductive process through which the invariable relation is arrived at (Sastri 1932: 206). Thus when one comes to have visual perception of smoke and fire, all particular smokes and fires are brought under its purview through the contact called generic (*sāmānya lakṣaṇa*). Accordingly, the relationship assumed between the perceived smoke and fire is extended to instances of smoke and fire not directly perceived (*Siddhāntamuktāvalī* I.65). On the other hand, Buddhist logicians like Diṅnāga and Dharmakīrti conceive of the relation in a negative way insisting that the *probans* should not exist in the absence of the *probandum* and describe the relation as invariableness (*avinābhāva*) (Sastri 1932: 207). They reject the scepticism aired by the Cārvākas and maintain that a general statement relating two things or events should be admitted to be true, when it is based on a universally accepted principle and made ground for everyday activity (Hiriyanna 1994: 200). They refer to the maxim that doubt is limited until it leads to self-contradiction or absurdity in practical absurdity (*vyāghātāvadhirāśaṅkā*). However, the Buddhists are keen to limit invariable concomitance to cases wherein the relationship is logically demonstrable. Accordingly, they maintain that two objects are invariably related only when they are having the relationship of identity (*tādātmya*) as in the case of copper and metal or causality (*tadutpatti*) as in the case of smoke and fire. To illustrate, one can infer that if the given thing is copper, it is also a metal, on the basis of the relationship of identity. Similarly, one can infer fire from smoke on the basis of causality, as smoke is caused by fire. The insistence on either of these relations means that the Buddhists do not consider the inference of one object from another, even if they are, for all practical purposes, concomitant, as in the case of the presence of horns in an animal which has cloven hoofs.

Nyāya and the Advaita

The Advaitins postulate the absolute as the ultimate reality and maintain that all other entities, including the material world and the individual selves are only appearances of the ultimate. This is not acceptable to the Naiyāyikas who accept the individual souls and the external world as real. They counter the argument of the Advaitins that the soul is identical with eternal knowledge. If so, the knowledge should have an object which is impossible. Nor can the individual souls, who are different from each other on the basis of knowledge, ignorance and happiness, be regarded as identical with *Brahman*. All such scriptures which maintain the identity of the individual souls and the supreme soul can be explained away in other ways also.

Nyāya and Vaiśeṣika

The Naiyāyikas, even when they are in agreement with most of the ontological views postulated by the Vaiśeṣikas, have a slight difference in the perception of many specific details. For example, both the systems agree on the fact that the qualities of colour, taste, smell and touch undergo change in earth due to a process called ripening (*pāka*), which is defined as the contact with a special kind of fire (*vijātīyatejas saṁyoga*). But the process is conceived in different manners by both the systems. According to the Vaiśeṣikas, when a clay is baked as in a pot, the aggregate is first disintegrated down to the atoms; then the concerned qualities like smell are destroyed in each atom, and a different quality is produced in their place. This view is known as Pīlupākavāda (the theory of the change of the atom). On the other hand, the Naiyāyikas do not accept the disintegration of the aggregate and postulate that the overall change in qualities take place in the aggregate itself. This theory is called Piṭharapākavāda (the theory of the change in the aggregate) (Sastri 1932: 90).

Another area in which the Naiyāyikas and the Vaiśeṣikas disagree is the number of the means of valid knowledge: while the Vaiśeṣikas accept only perception and inference as means of valid knowledge, the Naiyāyikas add analogy and verbal testimony to the list. The Vaiśeṣika's reluctance to accord validity to verbal testimony can be explained on the basis of their anti-Vedic stance in the original phase. In the later phase, they were, however inclined to include it under inference, along with analogy. The Naiyāyikas point out that there are certain difficulties in accepting this view as the perquisites of inference are wanting in verbal testimony, as there is no cognition of invariable concomitance (*vyāpti-jñāna*) either verbal testimony or analogy (*Siddhāntamuktāvalī*, pp. 140-41).

Nyāya and Mīmāṁsā

Both the Nyāya and the Mīmāṁsā share some common traits: both owe their origin to Vedic exegetics, even though at a later period, Nyāya became an autonomous branch of philosophy independent of Vedic exegetics. Again, both the systems believe in the reality of the external world, and hence can be described as realistic systems. The two schools also accept the view that the gross substances of the universe are made of atoms, even though the Mīmāṁsā concept of atom does not postulate a supersensory atom as distinct from the particles which are perceptible. But there are many differences between these schools in details. While the Mīmāṁsā postulate the eternality and self-validity of the Vedas which they believe to be not any product of human agency (*apauruṣeya*), the Naiyāyikas accept its validity since the Vedas constitute the words of the gods. Again, while the Mīmāṁsakas maintain that all knowledge is by nature valid, the Naiyāyikas take the position that the validity of knowledge has to be ascertained on the basis of fruitful activity (*saṁvādi-pravṛtti*). This is countered by the Mīmāṁsakas with the argument that the so-called verification itself is based on unverified knowledge: even a person dreaming about water can quench thirst by drinking it and so the fruitful activity is no guarantee for its being valid (Hiriyanna 1994: 108).

Another main difference between Mīmāṁsā and Nyāya is with regard to the number of means of valid knowledge (*pramāṇa*): while the Naiyāyikas confine themselves to four *pramāṇa*s, the Prābhākara Mīmāṁsakas add presumption (*arthāpatti*) also. This is assumed to account for the unstated fact which is assumed to resolve the apparent discrepancy between two statements which are equally valid. Thus, when we know that Devadatta is fat and Devadatta does not eat anything during the daytime, the only way to resolve the apparent discrepancy is to assume that he eats at night. The Naiyāyikas do not accept presumption as a separate *pramāṇa* as they feel that it could be included in inference, though the Mīmāṁsakas point out that the regular steps of inference are lacking in the presumption. The Bhāṭṭas, apart from presumption, accept non-apprehension (*anupalabdhi*) also as a *pramāṇa* to account for the cognition of non-existence, which is explained by the Naiyāyikas as an instance of direct perception.

6

The Hermeneutics of Śaṅkara
Some Methodological Musings

IN THE present paper, it is proposed to have a closer look at Śaṅkara as a commentator and exegesist and also to analyse the implicit methodology in his commentary on the *Brahmasūtras*. It is true that the stature of Śaṅkara as a philosopher per se has often eclipsed the fact that he wilfully chose the role of a commentator and not a propounder of an independent philosophy. It is also true that Advaita always being referred to as Śāṅkara Vedānta, it is difficult to view Śaṅkara as a mere commentator. In fact, Śaṅkara has been both eulogized and criticized for the alleged fact that he has propounded something new. Bhāskara, the propounder of Bhedābheda system, alleges that Advaita is a "fabrication of something new by him [Śaṅkara] through the exercise of his imagination" (Veezhinathan 1910: Intro, p. 1).

> I am writing a commentary on this *sūtra* in order to obstruct those commentators who have concealed its ideas and replaced them with their own. – Bhāskara 1915: 1

Nevertheless, the design of the discourse of Śaṅkara as enshrined in the *Bhāṣya* becomes unintelligible if we refuse to take it to be a commentary. In fact, Śaṅkara himself has been very careful to refrain from making the claim that his philosophy is something unknown to the tradition. In his commentary on the *Taittirīya Upaniṣad,* he makes it clear that the philosophy of Advaita has been handed down by tradition. Here he offers his salutations to the "ancient preceptors who have expounded the Upaniṣadic philosophy on the basis of Mīmāṁsā, Vyākaraṇa and Nyāya (I.I.2)". In the *Chāndogyopaniṣad Bhāṣya,* he refers to the continuous lineage in the transmission of the Upaniṣadic wisdom, Kaśyapa receiving it from God, and Manu receiving it from Kaśyapa and then transmitting it to humanity. There is even a strain of thought in Advaita that any interpretation of Upaniṣads without proper knowledge of the tradition is not authentic. Accordingly, Sureśvara, in his *Sūta Saṁhitā* (4.35.19) maintains:

> The knowledge of the teachings of the Upaniṣad imparted by one who does not know that traditional interpretation of the Upaniṣads is not knowledge, but exactly opposite of it. This is the considered view of the enlightened ones.[1]

Taking an analogy from the inviolable social norms of the times, he even maintains that without the traditional interpretation, it is not possible to attain self-realization.

> The knowledge of the traditional interpretation is necessary for self-realization just as the knowledge of one's lineage is necessary for one's marriage. – *Sūta Saṁhitā,* 4.35.19

In the *Gītābhāṣya*, Śaṅkara himself maintains that a person, who is ignorant of tradition, should be avoided like a fool, even when he knows all branches of knowledge.

From all this, it can be assumed that Śaṅkara had before him several intellectual tasks to perform to substantiate the doctrine of non-dualism with the attendant notions of *māyā* and the apparent transformation of the world of plurality. The Advaitic ideal of the realization of *Brahman* is an experience which negates the common-sense world view; ironically enough, it is the tools of the world of provisional reality which have to be pressed into service for advancing towards this goal. Śaṅkara reiterates that the only real means of valid knowledge in this respect is the scripture: it is only through the revealed scripture that one can attain the awareness of

[1] I have followed Veezhinathan's translation.

the Absolute, which is the first step leading to the realization of it in a unique experience transcending the distinctions of the knower and the known. In order to reinforce the doctrine of non-dualism, however, Śaṅkara finds it necessary to clear his way through the labyrinth of rival doctrines which propose alternate ontologies, epistemologies and visions of liberation. This dialectical method of argument and refutation, for which Śaṅkara is lauded in his life chronicles, is found more or less in a similar form in his *Bhāṣya*.

The opponent schools found to be necessary for refutation by Śaṅkara include the Cārvākas, various schools of Buddhism like the Sarvāstivāda, Vijñānavāda and Śūnyavāda, Jainism, Pūrva-Mīmāṁsā, Sāṁkhya, Yoga, Vaiśeṣika, Pāśupata, Pāñcarātra and Bhedābhedavāda (Sundaram 1981: 1-127). As is evident, these include both orthodox systems which swear by the allegiance to the Vedic scriptural authority and the heterodox systems which are not bound by such affiliation. The methodology adapted by Śaṅkara to refute the rival theories also varies from system to system. While countering the heterodox systems like the Cārvākas, Buddhists and Jainas, Śaṅkara seldom appeals to scriptural authority and refutes the doctrines of the rivals with logical arguments. In the case of theistic sects like the Pāśupatas and the Bhāgavatas, Śaṅkara takes up the sensitive issue of the limits of scriptural authority. He demonstrates that the alleged omniscience of seers like Kapila is based on the authority of the texts composed by them and as the texts themselves derive authority on the basis of the omniscience of their authors. In the case of the Pāñcarātra system, the claim that the Āgamas of the faith are even superior to the Vedas is regarded with suspicion by Śaṅkara. Coming to the Sāṁkhya and Mīmāṁsā schools, which claim that their doctrines are the authentic representations of the Vedic scriptural view, Śaṅkara uses hermeneutic tools to demonstrate that the import of the scripture is neither in the ritualistic acts, nor in the final dualism of the soul and the matter, as alleged by these systems.

An interesting example in the *Brahmasūtra* will give us insight to the integral vision of Śaṅkara encompassing the entire gamut of the scripture which he regards as authoritative. Commenting on the *sūtra* 1.1.2: *janmādyasya yataḥ*, Śaṅkara points out that this universe, characterized by name and form, is ultimately derived from the Absolute. Śaṅkara further maintains that such a world cannot be regarded as originating from anything else, like the *pradhāna* (primordial Nature), atoms, negation or some soul under worldly condition (*hiraṇyagarbha*).[2] It is significant that he uses the word *Īśvara* to denote the Absolute in this context, which could create some ambiguity related to a personal god. Following this thread, Śaṅkara further admits that this type of inference is used by those who believe in God as the cause of the world, intending the Naiyāyikas to establish the existence of God. In this context, Śaṅkara anticipates the objection by the opponent that the real intention of the author of the *Brahmasūtra* could also be this.

In replying this, Śaṅkara categorically states that the *Brahmasūtra* is meant for the stringing together of the flowers of the sentences of the end of the Vedas, meaning the Upaniṣads.[3] He further declares that the Absolute can be realized only after the conviction (*adhyavasāna*) arising from the deliberations [*vicāraṇa*] of the meaning of the sentences (of the scripture). Here Śaṅkara unambiguously declares his basic hypotheses in his hermeneutical enterprise, viz. that the corpus of the *Brahmasūtra* presents a unified vision rooted in the Upaniṣadic literature and that a proper comprehension of their meaning is absolutely necessary for the conviction which triggers of the realization of the Absolute. Śaṅkara concedes that means of valid knowledge like inference also are useful to strengthen the comprehension of the meaning of Vedāntic statements like *janmādyasya yataḥ*, provided that they do not go contrary to the Vedāntic statements themselves. Here he makes a methodological statement that logical reasoning (*tarka*) is acceptable as an ancillary to revealed scripture.[4] Here he

---

2 *Brahmasūtrabhāṣya*, 2000, p. 14.

3 *vedāntavākyakusumagrathanārthatvāt sūtrāṇām* – *Śāṅkarabhāṣya*, p. 135

4 *Śrutyaiva ca sahāyatvena tarkasyāpi abhyupetatvāt*
– *Śāṅkarabhāṣya* 1.1.3, p. 136

alludes to the story described in the *Chāndogyopaniṣad* of a person, who is blindfolded and led away from the country of Gāndhāra and left alone in a forest with his hands and feet tied up. He is rescued by some passersby, who free him and tell him the way to the Gāndhāra country. If he is intelligent (*paṇḍita*) enough, he can follow the instructions and reach the intended place. Similar is the predicament of a person steeped in ignorance to whom a teacher tells that he is *Brahman*. If he is intelligent enough to understand that and uses his reasoning faculty, he can attain *Brahman*.[5] However, Śaṅkara makes it amply clear that *Brahman*-hood is an experience proper because the true knowledge of it culminates in a unique experience; hence experience is itself the means of valid knowledge along with scripture and the like. Śaṅkara here makes a distinction between performable actions like the act of running on the one hand and existent realities like a tree on the other. Now a sacrifice and its attendant ancillaries, which are enjoined in scriptures, are tasks to be performed and the decision in this regard can be taken with the help of scriptures. Accordingly, one can perform a ritual or not. On the other hand, the Absolute is not an action to be accomplished at all. Whether one likes it or not, it is something already existent independent of the will of the perceiver, and its knowledge is to be determined on the basis of itself.

It is precisely here that Śaṅkara has to demonstrate that the methodology and perspective of Vedānta have to be different from that of Pūrva-Mīmāṁsā. Eventhough both of them swear by the validity of the Vedas, their approach is markedly different. The Mīmāṁsakas are mainly concerned with the injunctive part of the Vedic corpus and focus their attention on injunctions like "One desirous of heaven should perform sacrifice". They have little patience with mere descriptive statements like "Thou art that". Elaborating the meaning of the aphorism *śāstrayonitvād*, Śaṅkara refers to the view of Jaimini that the very purpose of the Veda is the enjoinment of action. Since the Upaniṣads do not contain any enjoinment of action, they will have to be regarded as of no use. If

---

[5] *Brahmasūtrabhāṣya*, 2000, p. 14 fn.

this is to be avoided, they will have to be regarded as ancillaries of some action through the prescription of the concerned agent in the form of an action like a specific ritual. Or else, the Upaniṣads will have to be taken as to enjoin meditation with reference to certain gods. The Mīmāṁsakas would not accept the argument that the Upaniṣads may be viewed as describing the nature of something the existence of which is already established; no such scriptural testimony is necessary for perceivable objects which are actualized through direct perception. Again, no aim of life is served by such descriptive statements which do not contain any reference to its acceptability or rejectability.

The usual methodology adopted by the Mīmāṁsakas when they encounter mere descriptive statements in the scriptures is to take them as explanatory statements (Arthavāda) which are then combined with some other injunctive statements. For example, a statement like "he wept" (*so arodīt*) in *Taittirīya Saṁhitā* 2.v.11 may not mean anything taken by itself. But when it is combined with an injunction, it may be taken to mean eulogizing something. Thus, in short, the Mīmāṁsakas contend that the only way in which the Upaniṣads can be harnessed is to treat them as supplementaries to the injunctive parts of the Vedas or as related to the meditations.

In countering theses objections, Śaṅkara demonstrates that the consensual import of the Upaniṣads is *Brahman*, as is exemplified by the *Brahmasūtra, tattu samanvayāt*. It is not proper to impute any other meaning to them. They cannot be taken to mean the delineation of the nature of the agent in the act of the performance of the sacrifice, as Upaniṣadic texts themselves deny any type of action, instrumentality and fruit of action to the Self. Here he has also to reject the view that if *Brahman* is something existent and not a task to be established like various rituals, it will be an object of senses like a pot. In this connection, he underlines an essential difference between the Absolute and ordinary objects of the objective world. One unique aspect of the Absolute is its identity with the self and this can be understood only with the help of scriptures like "Thou art that". This is not the case with ordinary objects which do not require such scriptural revelations for their cognition. Śaṅkara further tackles the fundamental problem posed by the Mīmāṁsakas that statements like "Though art that" are meaningless since they do not teach anything to be done or not to be done, as in the case of ritualistic enjoinments. He argues that if one realizes the true nature of the Absolute without any reference to things to be done or avoided, one realizes the final end of life consisting of the cessation of all miseries. Thus knowledge of the Absolute cannot be simply dismissed as of no practical use.

In this connection, Śaṅkara makes a distinction between Upaniṣadic statements which deal with the nature of various deities in connection with various types of meditation and the descriptive statements like "Thou art that". The latter are not to be confused with the former as they do not enjoin any type of meditation involving the Absolute. In fact, the Absolute cannot be regarded as an ancillary of the act of any meditation as it transcends any notion of duality involving the distinction between subject and object. More importantly, Śaṅkara insists that the Upaniṣadic portions explaining the nature of the Absolute cannot be treated on a par with instructional passages belonging to the ritualistic portions of the Vedic corpus. It is not proper to insist that the former and the latter are structurally identical and have to be regarded as subordinates to some specific action. If the Absolute were an ideal to be accomplished through some specific action, it would have to be considered as something which is transient, just like any other fruits of action like the heaven. In fact, all the prescriptive statements related to the Absolute have the limited purpose of removing the obstacles in the process.

Śaṅkara sums up the Vedāntic perspective in relation to the *sūtra, tattu samanvayāt,* making the following important clarifications:

1. All the Vedāntic statements have their import in the Absolute without any reference to any action to be performed.
2. The Sāṁkhyas interpret such statements as relating to concepts like *pradhāna*, taking the position that the absolute

reality is something cognized through methods like inference.

3. The logicians take the same statements as an aid to the inference of God and atoms, the efficient cause and the material cause of the universe.

To sum up, it can be seen that Śaṅkara counters rival doctrines using various methodological and hermeneutical tools depending on his exegetical tasks. He has to reject the ultimate postulation of any ontological entity like the *pradhāna* of the Sāṁkhyas and the atoms of the logicians. Śaṅkara also finds it necessary to unearth the basic difference between the ritualistic perspective of the Mīmāṁsakas and the revelatory perspective of the Vedāntins. While he finds it easy to counter rival heterodox doctrines on philosophical grounds, he has to resort to hermeneutic tools to clarify the Advaitic perspective and to reject the inadequacies of other possible interpretations of the Upaniṣadic portions of the scripture.

7

Kerala's Vedāntic Heritage

THOUGH known as the celebrated birthplace of Ādi-Śaṅkara, it has always been pointed out that when it comes to the question of the reception of Vedānta, Kerala has not been as enthusiastic as in the case of the sister system of Pūrva-Mīmāṁsā. Thus even Vatakkamkur Rajarajavarma, the doyen of Kerala Sanskrit literary history, who does not subscribe to the theory, concedes:

> It is doubtless that Brahma-Mīmāṁsā, consisting of knowledge, had a definite place in Kerala. But it was not that much high as in the case of other systems. – Rajarajavarma 1997, vol. I: 25

Hailed as the land of ritual (*karmabhūmi*), Kerala has been a fertile soil so far as the growth and development of ritualistic precepts and practices are concerned, including the two schools of Pūrva-Mīmāṁsā. It will be interesting to probe as to how the uneasy relationship between the protagonists of ritual and spiritual wisdom has been responsible for the alleged lukewarm reception of Advaitic thought in the households of the Nampoothiri brahmaṇa of Kerala, even though the great Ādi-Śaṅkara was himself a scion of the community.

However, all this does not mean that Kerala has been totally lagging behind in the development of Vedāntic thought. Of the eighteen *sabhā-maṭhas* which were functioning in Kerala for the propagation of Vedic and Śāstric studies, three were earmarked for Vedāntic studies while the Bhāṭṭa system of Mīmāṁsā had six, the Prābhākara system another six and Vyākaraṇa three. Vedānta was also represented in the famous scholarly assemblage of Ravatī Paṭṭattānam of Calicut along with Vyākaraṇa and schools of Mīmāṁsā. Last, impact of the life and works of the great Śaṅkarācārya on Kerala's philosophical thought cannot be belittled as is evidenced by the bulk of works produced here in Vedānta and the type of institutional support Vedānta received in Kerala due to his influence.

Śaṅkara is generally assigned to the eighth century CE by the great majority of scholars on the basis of internal and external evidences. Kunjunni Raja points out that Śaṅkara is later than Bhartṛhari, Diṅnāga, Gauḍapāda, Dharmakīrti and Kumārila whom he quotes. This would place him after 650 CE. Since Vācaspati Miśra wrote his commentary on his *Bhāṣya* in 841 CE, Śaṅkara, who must be earlier to him by one or two generations, cannot be later than 800 CE. Śāntarakṣita (705-62 CE) and Kamalaśīla (713-63 CE), who introduced Buddhism to Tibet and who discuss Upaniṣadvāda do not mention Śaṅkara at all. From all this, we can safely conclude that Śaṅkara must have composed his works towards the close of the eighth century CE (Kunjunni Raja 1982: 72). It is well known that Śaṅkara left Kerala and studied Advaita at the feet of Govindācārya and later, he travelled all over India to debate with scholars and finally to ascend the Śāradāpīṭha in Kashmir.

There is no unanimity among scholars about the number of works actually written by Śaṅkara. Those ascribed to him amount to 400 in number, and many of them may be spurious. But the genuine works of Śaṅkara definitely include the celebrated *bhāṣyas* on the ten principal Upaniṣads, the *Brahmasūtras* and, in all probability, the *Bhagavadgītā* also, which constitutes the three canonical texts (*prasthānatraya*) of Vedānta. Apart from these, the *Upadesasāhasrī* which gives us a terse account of the Advaitic tenets, the *Vivekacūḍāmaṇi, Aparokṣānubhūti, Vākyavṛtti, Svātmanirūpaṇa, Ātmabodha* and innumerable *stotra* works are attributed to Śaṅkara, and many of them may be quite genuine works of him. The main refrain of Śaṅkara throughout is the basic identity of the Absolute and the individual souls. Even while remaining a staunch non-dualist, he composed *stotras* on deities like Viṣṇu and Śiva from the point of view of duality to address to the concerns of the laity, evidently to guide them to the ultimate realization of the Absolute in a step by step manner. One of the outstanding contributions of Śaṅkara as a philosopher and polemist is that he could effectively counter the ontological and epistemological positions of his rivals including the Mīmāṁsakas, Sāṁkhyas, Vaiśeṣikas, Naiyāyikas, adherents of different schools of Buddhism, Jainas, Cārvākas, Bhāgavatas and Pāśupatas. Śaṅkara recognized different levels of experience to account for the variety of contradictory world views. Another great attraction of Śaṅkara was his clarity of thought and conviction and his capacity to present the most abstract thought in a convincing and clear-cut manner with the help of worldly maxims and striking illustrations. His philosophy was inclusive in the sense that he could explain the positions of rival schools from the perspective of the all-comprehensive non-dual position from which he looked at phenomenon.

Coming to the post-Śaṅkara period, tradition maintains that Padmapādācārya, the first disciple of Śaṅkara, was a Keralite. He appears to be a Nampoothiri brahmaṇa who belonged to Vemannu Amsam in Alattur initiated by Śaṅkara in Benares. It is generally believed that Śaṅkara himself commissioned him to write a gloss on his *Brahmasūtrabhāṣya* eventhough initially he wanted Sureśvara to do so. The story goes that Padmapāda composed the work in his native village, and when he embarked upon a pilgrimage to Rāmeśvaram, the Nampoothiri brahmaṇas of the village, who were staunch supporters of Mīmāṁsā tradition, took the work from him and later consumed it to flames. It is believed that Śaṅkara himself, who had read the first five *pādas* of the work recited that portion from his memory and thus restituted the portion, which came to be known as the *Pañcapādikā*. It is the oldest gloss on Śaṅkara's *Bhāṣya* and it has a gloss called the *Pañcapādikāvivaraṇa* by Prakāśātman. It is the nucleus text of the Vivaraṇa school of Advaita as distinct from the Bhāmatī school of Vācaspati Miśra (Nampoothiri 1996: 61). The main difference between the two schools is that while the Bhāmatī school maintains that ignorance (*avidyā*) has *Brahman* as its object and is located in the individual soul, the Vivaraṇa school is of the view that both the locus and content of it are *Brahman* itself. The available portion of the *Pañcapādikāvivaraṇa* covers only the four *sūtra* (*catussūtrī*) portion of the *Bhāṣya*, but there are indications in the text itself that the author wanted to cover the entire text.

Another great Advaitin of Kerala is Sarvajñayati alias Sarvajñātman, who seems to have lived during the regime of Manukūlāditya of the tenth century. His *Saṁkṣepaśārīraka* consisting of 1,240 verses, divided into four chapters, is a lucid exposition of the views of Śaṅkara as expounded in his *bhāṣya*. Tradition holds that Sarvajñayati was a disciple of Sureśvarācārya, who was a direst disciple of Śaṅkara but this view is now challenged by scholars. The author himself at the end of his *Samkṣepaśārīraka* refers to Padmanābha of Śrīpadmanābha Temple of Trivandrum. It seems that he was a "Puṣpāñjali Svāmiyar" of Padamanābha Svāmī Temple of Trivandrum and a disciple of Deveśvara and he belonged to the late part of tenth century. He explains the relationship between *Brahman* and *jīva* on the basis of reflection theory (Pratibimbavāda). The *Pramāṇalakṣaṇa*, his another work, deals with the various means of valid knowledge accepted by Advaitins. The *Pañcaprakriyā* is another work of the author in five sections, dealing with the functions of word and other epistemological matters and the *mahāvākyas* of Vedānta.

The next important author in the Advaitic tradition of Kerala is Nr̥siṁhācārya, who seems to be the pontiff at the Tekke Svāmiyar Maṭham of Trichur. His *Tattvabodhinī* is a commentary on the *Saṁkṣepaśārīraka*. His other works include the *Advaitadīpikā, Tattvadīpana, Advaitavāda*, commentary on the *Śvetāśvataropaniṣadbhāṣya* of Śaṅkara, *Bhedādhikāra, Nr̥siṁhavijñāpana, Vedāntaratnakośa, Bhāvaprakāśikā* commentary on Prakāśātman's *Vivaraṇa* and the *Vācārambhaṇa* commentary on the sixth *khaṇḍa* of *Chāndogyopaniṣad.* Though not a very original thinker, he emphasized on the central theme of Advaita, consisting of the identity of *Brahman* and *ātman.* He also identifies self with bliss itself.

The Advaitic tradition continues with Nṛsiṁhaprajñayati, who was probably the pontiff of the Svāmiyar Maṭham of Trichur. His main works include a commentary on the *Bṛhadāraṇyakopaniṣad,* and a commentary on Sureśvara's *Vārttika* on the *Bṛhadāraṇyakabhāṣya.* He wrote another work also, entitled *Brahmagītavyākhyā.* Another great scholar was Vedānanda, who wrote an elaborate commentary called the *Sambanddhokti* on the *Saṁkṣepaśārīraka* of Sureśvara. Kṛṣnabhūtiyati, who belonged to the fifteenth century, is another author who wrote two works, viz. the *Śārīrakamīmāṁsāsaṁgraha* also known as the *Śāstrasaṁgraha* and the *Brahmasūtrādhikaraṇanyāyānukramaṇikā.* We know very little about Pūrṇavidyā Muni, the author of the *Pañcaprakriyāvyākhyā* except that his preceptor's name was one Vedapūrṇa. Kṛṣṇānanda, who came to Kerala from Nāgapura on the banks of Gaṅgā who was the preceptor of Rāghavānanda, appears to have composed two Advaitic works, viz. commentaries on the *Advaitarasamañjarī* and Śaṅkara's *Ātmabodha.* Kṛṣṇalīlāśuka, the celebrated author of the *Śrīkṛṣṇakarṇāmṛta* wrote a commentary on the *Kenopaniṣadbhāṣya* called the *Śaṅkarahṛdayaṅgama.* In this work, he tries to reconcile the two versions of the *Śāṅkarabhāṣya* on the Upaniṣad. Another scholar is Durgāprasādayati, a saint in Tekke Svāmiyar Maṭham at Trichur, identified with Nārāyaṇapriyayati, who wrote the *Sneha* commentaries on Bodhāyana's *Kaivalyanavanīta* and *Advaitaprakāśa.*

A great writer on Advaita from Kerala of the succeeding times is Rāghavānanda, a poet, preceptor and commentator. He was a student of Kṛṣṇānanda whom he refers to in most of his works and who, according to the traditional *kali* chronogram *puṇyāṭavyām yatiḥ syād,* belonged to the fourteenth century CE (Nampoothiri 1996: 95). Some people identify him with Kokkunnāth Śivayogin of Taliparamba (Saratchandran 1997: 109), but this is rejected by Ullūr who maintains that he was born at a place near Bhāratappuzha.

His works include the *Kṛṣṇapadī*, a commentary on the *Bhāgavata Purāṇa*, the *Vivaraṇa*, a commentary on the *Paramārthasāra* of Śeṣa, the *Sarvamatasaṁgraha* or *Sarvasiddhāntasaṁgraha*, a digest of all systems of philosophy, the *Vidyārcanāmañjarī, Māṇḍūkyopaniṣad-bhāṣyārthasaṁgraha, Vidyāmṛtavarṣiṇī, Tattvārthacandrikā, Mīmāṁsāstavaka, Dīdhiti* commentary on the *Mīmāṁsāsūtra* of Jaimini, commentary on Padmapāda's *Prapañcasāravyākhyā* and *Tattvārṇava* commentary on Vācaspati's *Sāṁkhyatattvakaumudī*. Unfortunately, all these works are lost.

Other Vedāntic scholars of the pre-modern Kerala include Vināyaka (fourteenth century), the author of *Siddhāntapañjara*, Vāsudevayati, the author of *Vedāntaprakaraṇa*, Devanārāyaṇa, the king of Ambalapuzha and the author of *Vedāntaratnamālā* which is an elaborate commentary on the first verse of the *Bhāgavata*, Brahmānandayati, the author of *Bṛhadbrahmānandīya*, Bodhānanda, the author of *Bodhānandagītā* which is a metrical summary of the *Upaṇisadbhāṣyas* of Śaṅkara, Vāsudeva Svāmī, who flourished in the seventeenth century and was the author of *Vivekasāra*, a lucid treatise on Vedānta. The traditional Vedāntic scholarship flourished albeit in a modest way even until recent times with a host of scholars writing on different aspects of Advaita. These include the Anantanārāyaṇa Śāstrī of the eighteenth century who wrote a commentary on the *Viṣṇusahasranāma*, Tekketam Svāmiyar, the author of the allegorical drama called *Pūrṇapuruṣārthacandrodaya*, and the anonymous author of *Haṁsasandeśa* which is a philosophical message poem. While Vīrakeralavarma Tampurān (1764–1828) of Cochin was a follower and patron of the Madhva school of Dvaita, Rāmavarma Mahārāja of Cochin (1851–1930) was a staunch admirer of Advaita and he wrote a summary for the *Vedāntaparibhāṣā* entitled *Vedāntaparibhāṣāsaṁgraha*. Ādinārāyaṇa, who flourished in the beginning of the twentieth century wrote three Advaita works: viz. the *Caturvedamahāvākyaṭīkā*, called *Cintāmaṇi, Advaitāmṛtasāraka* and *Ṣaḍviṁśadavaitatattvamālikā*, but no personal details of the author are available. Easwaran Nampoothiri conjectures that he belonged to Mannarkudi or to its precincts (Nampoothiri 1996: 128).

It is interesting to note that Advaita philosophy which was confined to scholarly circles became a powerful ideology at the time of the national renaissance in India's struggle against foreign domination. The powerful stimulus for this philosophical rejuvenation came from great saints like Svami Vivekananda, who reinterpreted Vedānta on the basis of the basic equality of human beings irrespective of caste and status. Thus Advaita which was accessible only to higher echelons of society was claimed to be a universal religion cutting across class, caste, creed, region and language. In Kerala, this paradigmatic shift in the perceptions of Advaita was brought about by great social reformers like Śrīvidyādhirāja Cattampi Svāmikal, Śrīnārāyaṇa Guru, Vāgbhaṭānanda and Ālattūr Brahmānanda Śivayogī. The Sanskrit works of Cattampi Svāmikal (1853–1923) include the *Vedādhikāranirūpaṇa, Cidākāśālaya, Sarvamatasāmarasya, Brahmatattvanirbhāsa, Stavaratnahārāvalī, Tarkarahasyaratna, Paramaśivastava* and *Advaitapañjara*. Besides, he composed the *Mokṣapradīpakhaṇḍanam, Prācīnamalayālam* and *Advaitacintāpaddhati* in Malayalam. He refutes the argument that śūdras do not have any eligibility to study Vedas and Vedānta and asserts that non-brāhmaṇas have equal rights to study Veda and Tantra like brāhmaṇas. He argued that it is the preponderance of the *sattva, rajas* and *tamas* which determines the eligibility of a person and not simply his birth. In Śrīnārāyaṇa Guru (1857–1929) Vedānta develops into a powerful tool to fight against caste oppression. His masterly treatises the *Brahmavidyāpañcaka, Ātmopadeśaśataka, Advaitadīpikā, Daivadaśaka, Jñānavārttāmañjarī Brahmavidyāpañcaka, Municaryāpañcaka* and *Darśanamālā* expound the Advaitic thought developing it into its logical conclusions. Śrīnārāyaṇa Guru used Advaita, which proclaims the essential unity of all phenomena as the philosophical basis for his staunch position that caste and creed have no place in an ideal society. Vāgbhaṭānanda (1885–1939), a staunch advocate of Advaita from north Kerala, was the founder of Ātmavidyāsaṅgha and a strong opponent of idol worship. Brahmānanda Śivayogī (1852–1929), who fought against all superstitions underlined the blissful nature of spiritual experience.

A review of the Advaitic tradition of Kerala reveals that despite the preponderance of rituals and the Mīmāṁsā tradition, Advaita was not completely sidelined. On the other hand, we see the tradition cultivated zealously by various *sabhā-maṭha*s and individual scholars who were mostly saints themselves. The Advaitic dictum, *vyavahāre bhāṭṭa nayaḥ* must have probably helped the Advaitic thought to develop its epistemology in Kerala which was a fertile soil for the growth of both the schools of Mīmāṁsā. Tradition was kept alive by recapitulations through commentaries and digests and we do not see any new thought form emerging like the Vivaraṇa *paddhati* or Bhāmatī *paddhati*. But it is also interesting to note that unlike in other parts of south India, non-Śaṅkara traditions like the Dvaita or Viśiṣṭādvaita did not have any serious impact in Kerala and this may be due to the impact of Advaita. Great devotional poets like Melputtūr Nārāyaṇa Bhaṭṭa subscribe to a theistic form of Advaita and feel no contradiction in combining theism and absolutism. Finally, with the advent of renaissance, Advaita emerged in Kerala as a powerful tool for social reform in tune with the emerging aspirations of an egalitarian society.

8

Contribution of Kerala to Mīmāṁsā Philosophy

KERALA is acclaimed as the birthplace of Ādi-Śaṅkara, whose philosophy upheld spiritual wisdom (*jñāna*) above *karman* (ritual). But it is also known as the land of rituals (*karmabhūmi*) in view of its close association with Vedic rituals from time immemorial. Tradition maintains that sacrificial rite was in vogue in Kerala for centuries and when it became extinct, it was the legendary Mezhattur Agnihotri who revived it around fourth century CE. He is supposed to have himself performed a hundred sacrifices. There are plenty of documents indicating that sacrifices like Aśvamedha, Agniṣṭoma and Atirātra were performed here from ancient times. The rich ritualistic tradition may be the reason for the prevalence of Pūrva-Mīmāṁsā philosophy in Kerala down the ages. It is an incontrovertible fact that rituals and ritualistic philosophy enjoyed more popularity and institutional support here than asceticism and Vedāntic philosophy.

The Mīmāṁsā philosophy has a hoary history in Kerala. There is a reference to a certain Bhavadāsa in Śabarasvāmi's *Bhāṣya* on the *Mīmāṁsāsūtra* and it is generally believed that he was a Keralite "since this name is current only among Namputiri brahmaṇas" (Iyer 1976: 69). He is the author of *Pūrvamīmāṁsāsūtravṛtti*, a commentary on Jaimini's *sūtras*. The work is not available now, but mentioned by Devasvāmin of tenth century.

Tradition mentions that Prabhākara, the propounder of the Prābhākara system of Pūrva-Mīmāṁsā, was a Keralite. Prabhākara, also known as Prabhākara Miśra, belonged to 620-80 CE. According to the *Keralotpatti* legends, his sandals were being worshipped at Udayatuṅgeśvara. He is supposed to have belonged to Paṭiññāre Kūttulli Illam in Śukapuram village of Malappuram district. Prabhākara refers to the matriarchal system of inheritance, a feature of some castes of Kerala. He also holds the views of Bhavadāsa against those of Kumārila Bhaṭṭa, his arch rival. However, according to some other traditions, he belonged to Mithilā. According to a manuscript in the Asiatic Society of Bengal, he was the son of Vibhākara, the chief minister to the king of Dakṣiṇakosala (Iyer 1976: 67). Prabhākara is the author of two commentaries: the *Bṛhatī* and *Laghvī* on the *Śābarabhāṣya*. It is indisputable that the Prābhākara system was very popular in Kerala, though somewhat less in degree in comparison with the Bhāṭṭa system. Hence there may be some element of truth in the traditional belief that he was a Keralite.

Vatakkamkur Rajarajavarma, however, records the traditional belief that it was the Bhāṭṭa school which made its presence felt in Kerala first. The following verse in the *Kokilasandeśa* of Uddaṇḍa Śāstrī suggests that it was a king of northern Kerala called Hariścandra who propagated the Bhāṭṭa system in Kerala.

yeṣām vaṁśe samājani hariścandranāmā narendraḥ
pratyāpattiḥ pataga yadupajñam ca kaumarilānām |
yuddhe yeṣāmhitahataye caṇḍikā sanidhatte
teṣāmeṣām stutiṣu na bhavetkasya vaktram pavitram ||

– Unni 1997: I.45

Probably the Prābhākara system received footage at a later period. The Bhāṭṭas seem to have enjoyed more popularity in Kerala than the Prābhākaras. Anyway, the Bhāṭṭas and the Prābhākaras got equal status in the assignment of various centres of learning called *sabhā-maṭhas* in medieval Kerala. Among the eighteen ones, six went to the Bhāṭṭas, six to the Prābhākaras, the rest being shared by the Vedāntins and Vedānta equally.

The Mīmāṁsā tradition in Kerala was centred on certain families and the most important of them is that of the Payyūr Bhaṭṭas. It is believed that not less than nine members of the family were included in the "eighteen and half" poets (*patineṭṭarakkavikal*) patronized by King Mānavikrama, the Zamorin of Calicut who reigned in the second half of the fifteenth century CE. It is difficult to identify the names of all the scholars since the family uses only the names *ṛṣi* or *parameśvara* to denote its members and there were more than one having the same name. The *Uṇṇunīlisandeśa* of the fourteenth century CE refers to the poetic talents of the Payyūr Bhaṭṭas in part II, verse 14, through the expression, *Paṭṭam payyūr kavita cuvayilla* (Kunjunni Raja 1980: 90). Uddaṇḍa Śāstrī, the famous scholar poet, who adorned the court of the Zamorin, himself was one of the eighteen and half poets, and Kākkaśśeri Bhaṭṭa, who was a rival of the former, both pay glowing tributes to the Payyūr Bhaṭṭas. Uddaṇḍa, in his play, the *Mallikāmāruta* refers to *ṛṣi* as *traividyeśo maharṣirnirūpamamahimā yaddhite jāgarūkaḥ* and to *parameśvara* as *kṛtameva tad mīmāṁsācakravartinā maharṣiputreṇa parameśvareṇa.* It is really interesting to note that Uddaṇḍa, who looked down upon native scholars with disdain, held the Payyūr Bhaṭṭas in high esteem. In his *Kokilasandeśa,* Uddaṇḍa refers to even the group of parrots in the house of *maharṣi*, who is the preceptor of "two Mīmāṁsās (meaning the Pūrva and Uttara Mīmāṁsā) belonging to the place Raṇakhala (a Sanskritized form of Porkkalam near Kunnamkulam of central Kerala), ready to confront scholars who come for arguments.

kiñcitpūrvam raṇakhalabhuvi śrīmadadhyakṣayedhāḥ
tanmīmāṁsādvayakulaguroḥ sadma puṇyam maharṣeḥ ।
vidvadvṛnde vivāditumanasyāgate yatraśāśvad
vyāakhyāśālāvalabhinilyastiṣṭhate kīrasamkhaḥ ॥

– Unni 1997: I.79

There is a temple dedicated to Goddess Gopālikā near Porkkalam who seems to be the family deity of the Payyur Bhaṭṭas. However, in the *Cakorasandeśa* written by one of the members of the family of the Payyur Bhaṭṭas, there is a mention of Vedāraṇya, near Tirunava as the place of the Payyūr Bhaṭṭas. On the basis of this, K. Kunhan Raja maintains that the original place of the Bhaṭṭas was at that place and later they shifted to Porkkalam.

Vatakkamkur Rajarajavarma conjectures that the famous Mīmāṁsā scholar Maṇḍana Miśra was a member of the Payyur family, but this seems to be far-fetched. The verse quoted by Vatakkamkur in support of his argument:

maṇḍanacaryakr̥tayo yesvadhiyanta kr̥tsnasaḥ ।
tadvaṁśyena mayapyeśa racitaradhyādevataḥ ।।

simply states that the works of Maṇḍana were taught in their entirety in the Payyur family.

Among the Payyur Bhaṭṭas, the earliest one known to us through literary references in *r̥ṣi* I, but no work written by him is available now. Parameśvara I, the son of *r̥ṣi* I, is the author of *Nyāyasamuccaya* and two commentaries on the *Nyāyakaṇikā* of Vācaspati Miśra called the *Jusadhvamkaraṇī* and *Svaditamkaraṇī.* His grandson Parameśvara II wrote the *Gopālikā* commentary on Maṇḍana Miśra's *Sphoṭasiddhi, Tattvavibhāvanā* on Vācaspati Miśra's *Tattvabindu* and commentaries on Cidānanda's *Nititattvāvirbhāva* and Maṇḍana's *Vibhramaviveka.* Parameśvara III, his grandson, wrote *Jaiminīyasūtrārthasaṁgraha* and *Mīmāṁsāślokavārttikakāśikā-vyākhyā.* Vasudeva (fifteenth century CE), the brother of Parameśvara III, is the author of *Kaumārilayuktimālā.*

A great work in Bhāṭṭa Mīmāṁsā produced by Kerala is the *Mānameyodaya* jointly authored by Melputtūr Nārāyaṇa Bhaṭṭa and Nārāyaṇa Paṇḍit. Divided into *māna* (means of knowledge) and *meya* (content of knowledge) portions, it is an elementary treatise on the fundamental epistemological and ontological principles of the Bhāṭṭa system. It seems that the work which had to be left incomplete by Melputtur with its *Māna* portion, probably due to his death, was completed by Nārāyaṇa Paṇḍit at the instance of the Zamorin of Calicut. The work gained an all-India popularity and has been studied as a basic textbook on the Bhāṭṭa system. In the words of Kuppuswami Sastri:

> Within a brief compass, in a style which is at once lucid and terse, this work gives an able and well-grounded exposition of the leading tenets of the philosophical system of the Bhāṭṭa school, and adds comparative and critical remarks when required with particular reference to the corresponding tenets of the other systems of Indian philosophical thought chiefly the Prābhākara, Nyāya, Advaita and Bauddha.[1]

This should serve as an epitome of the present brief survey.

---

1 Foreword to the edition of *Mānameyodaya* by Kunhan Raja et al., quoted by Kunjunni Raja, 1980: 139.

9

Influence of Pūrva-Mīmāṁsā on Alaṁkāraśastra

As THE saying *sarvapāṣadam idam śāstram*, declares, Alaṁkāraśāstra is eclectic in nature. While it has no exclusive ontological or epistemological positions to stick to, it freely makes use of the tenets of other disciplines like grammar and logic. There is probably nothing wrong about it, since poeticians, confined to the world of creative writings, are not generally expected to address themselves the ultimate questions of metaphysics. This gives them a certain freedom to adopt concepts from sister disciplines without compromising their basic positions. The borrowing of concepts does not affect the vigour or validity of poetics. However, we may wonder whether Pūrva-Mīmāṁsā, the Indian science of hermeneutics, has exerted any influence on it at all. Unlike the Nyāya or Vedānta, Pūrva-Mīmāṁsā has not been a dominant philosophical system from second millennium, when Alaṁkāraśāstra developed its linguistic speculations and probably required reinforcement of its positions from other disciplines. But our scepticism in this regard is misplaced. Pūrva-Mīmāṁsā, at least its language philosophy, has exerted considerable influence on Alaṁkāraśāstra which evolved its own linguistic positions with the advent of the *dhvani* doctrine.

The linguistic thought of both the Prābhākaras and Bhāṭṭas has been used by the Ālaṁkārikas to define their own positions and to clarify their positions. This is not to suggest that the Ālaṁkārikas, as a tribe, have borrowed the interpretive tools of the Mīmāṁsakas indiscriminately to serve their purposes. In fact, most of the great poeticians of the formative period of Alaṁkāraśāstra which roughly correspond to ninth to twelfth centuries CE, were independent thinkers and they disagreed with each other on many points. Their attitude to Pūrva-Mīmāṁsā can be described as eclectic and tentative. While they were happy to accept its dicta when they found them to be supportive to their own theories, they also expected the Pūrva-Mīmāṁsā to accept their positions in linguistic problems like the acceptance of suggestion.

I

This new interface was heralded by Ānandavardhana, who, in his *Dhvanyāloka* postulated a new function for poetic language called *vyañjanā*, to account for the comprehension of the suggested meaning which could not be explained by *abhidhā* and *lakṣaṇā*, the primary and secondary powers of language, takes the stand that suggestion is an adventitious (*aupādhika*) function of language and avers that it has to be accepted by the Mīmāṁsakas who make distinction between human (*pauruṣeya*) and suprahuman (*apauruṣeya*) languages. The latter, being impersonal, is free from the usual blemishes attributable to the former like the imperfection of the speaker. But this will be possible if Mīmāṁsakas accept adventitious functions like *vyañjanā* to account for the manifestation of "impurities" like the speaker's intention in ordinary human language. In other words, the acceptance of the suggestive power of language (*vyañjanā*) over and above the power of expression and indication is in consonance with the position of the Mīmāṁsakas that scriptural language is qualitatively different from ordinary language (Ānandavardhana 1940: 438).

The necessity of the acceptance of *vyañjanā* by both the schools of Pūrva-Mīmāṁsā is elaborated at greater length by Abhinavagupta. Interestingly, Abhinavagupta does not take side in the dispute between the Prābhākaras and the Bhāṭṭas about the cognition of the meaning of a sentence, viz. whether syntactical relations are cognized before the cognition of the meaning of individual words (Anvitābhidhānavāda), held by the former or after it (Abhihitānvayavāda) a view held by the Bhāṭṭas. The former would argue that a sentence first of all will convey its syntactical relations through a unified sentence structure followed by an overall unified meaning. The Bhāṭṭas contend that the words individually convey their meanings first and the syntactical relation is comprehended only afterwards. According to Abhinavagupta, whether one accepts the Abhihitānvayavāda of the Bhāṭṭas or the Anvitābhidhānavāda of Prābhākaras, the comprehension of the suggested meaning will be possible only when one accepts *vyañjanā*.[1] Abhinavagupta maintains that neither denotation (*abhidhā*) nor purport (*tātparya-śakti*) can explain the comprehension of the suggested meaning, which is explainable only on the basis of *vyañjanā*. In *anvitābhidhāna*, the syntactical relation is conveyed by the sentence at the very outset; hence no power is necessary for its comprehension. *Abhidhā* gives rise to the primary meaning. If there is any discrepancy in it, *lakṣaṇā* is resorted to clear it. But neither of these functions is capable of explaining the suggested meaning, and hence the Prābhākaras who subscribe to this view have also to accept the process of *vyañjanā*. Thus, in short, Abhinavagupta and the other poeticians following him conceive of a four-tier model in the case of Bhāṭṭas' system and a three-tier model in the case of the Prābhākaras to accommodate *dhvani*.

---

[1] There is a slight discrepancy in the representation of the Bhāṭṭa view by Abhinavagupta here. As pointed out by Kunjunni Raja, Bhāṭṭas accept *lakṣaṇā* as the power responsible for the cognition of the sentence meaning from the meaning of the individual words. However, Abhinavagupta argues that *tātparya-śakti* is the power postulated by the Bhāṭṭas for the comprehension of the sentence meaning. Actually, *tātparya-śakti* was actually postulated by Jayanta Bhaṭṭa, the famous Naiyāyika. See Kunjunni Raja, 1963, *Indian Theories of Meaning*, pp. 213-24.

Abhinavagupta further refutes the position of the Prābhākaras that the actual intended meaning of the sentence is got automatically irrespective of the expressed meaning. Abhinavagupta points out that the Prābhākaras who subscribe to Anvitābhidhānavāda liken the operation of the word to that of an arrow which, once shot, does not rest until its final target is reached. According to Abhinavagupta, this cannot be true. We have to assume cause–effect relationship (*nimitta-nimitti-bhāva*) between the expressed and the suggested meaning. Otherwise the Mīmāṁsākas cannot explain their well-known positions like the difference between the expressed and the secondary meaning (which are cause and effect) and also the progressive weakness (*pāradaurbalya*) of the six *pramāṇa*s like *śruti* and *liṅga*, which help one to determine the purport of an injunctive statement against the background of conflicting possibilities of interpretation as well as ambiguity.

Prābhākaras maintain that the effect (*naimittika*), i.e. the suggested meaning, does not require any convention (*saṅketa*) and only the cause (*nimitta*), i.e. the conventional meaning, requires it. Thus, whereas the conventional meaning requires the knowledge of the convention on the part of the hearer, no such preconditions are necessary in the case of the suggested meaning. If this were right, it will reverse the normal order of the cognition of the meaning; the suggested meaning will be cognized first, as it does not require any convention, to be followed by the expressed meaning which requires the convention. Abhinavagupta jocularly remarks that Mīmāṁsakas would be maintaining that the great grandson will be the precursor of the father if this order is accepted.[2] In short, we cannot assume the cognition of an intended meaning totally disregarding the natural cognition process in language where we get a conventional meaning at the very outset from which other meanings emerge.

---

[2] *nūnam mīmāṁsakasya prapautram prati naimittikatvam abhimatam*

– Ānandavardhana 1940: 66

II

It seems that *dhvani* doctrine was severely criticized by Bhaṭṭanāyaka, an aesthetician who made use of Mīmāṁsā concepts in the formulation of his own theory. Bhaṭṭanāyaka maintains that the poetic language has actually three powers: that of denotation (*abhidhā*), that of universalization (*bhāvanā*) and that of enjoyment (*bhojakatva*). These are mentioned in some verses ascribed to him by Abhinavagupta in the *Abhinavabhāratī* (1975: 277).

abhidhā bhāvanā caiva tatadbhogīkṛtireva ca |
abhidhādhāmatām yāte śabdārthālamkṛtī tataḥ ||
bhāvanābhāvya eṣo 'pi sṛṅgārādigaṇo bhaved |
tadbhogīkṛtirūpeṇa vyāpyate siddhimān naraḥ ||

Accordingly, the power of denotation gives the literal meaning, and the power of *bhāvanā* makes the *rasa* enjoyable. Here the concept of *bhāvanā* is definitely taken from the Mīmāṁsakas who maintain that a statement like "One should perform a sacrifice" (*yajeta svargakāmaḥ*) gives rise to two operative functions called *śābdī* and *ārthī bhāvanā*. *Bhāvanā* is defined as "the operation on the part of the agent conducive to the production of the thing to be produced" (*bhavitur bhāvanānukūlo bhāvayitur vyāpāraviśeṣo bhāvanā*). It is either a word power (*śābdī-bhāvanā*) motivating the listener or a material power (*ārthī-bhāvanā*) existing in actual objects. The former is related to the linguistic comprehension of an injunction, while the latter deals with the operative part of the real task to be accomplished. Taking the *śābdī-bhāvanā* first, the injunction "he desirous of heaven should sacrifice" (*yajeta svargakāmaḥ*) has an injunctive mood which contains a word power motivating the listener to perform a sacrifice. It answers three queries. The first one is, "What is to be accomplished (*kim bhāvayet*)", the answer being the sacrifice, the content of the *ārthī-bhāvanā*, the material power. The next query is: "By what means is it to be accomplished (*kena bhāvayet*)?" Here the answer is that the volition for the performance of sacrifice, the accomplishment desired, happens through knowledge on the part of the reader about the features of the injunctive mood. In other words, a person aware of the implications of the injunctive mood, on hearing the above statement, will understand that the statement impels him to perform the prescribed sacrifice. The final query is "how is the accomplishment being done? (*katham bhāvayet*)". The answer is the greatness (*prāśastya*) of the sacrifice. One becomes enthused of the performance when one listens to the stories and statements which glorify the particular sacrifice. Coming to the *ārthī-bhāvanā*, the motivating factor is the attainment of heaven, the means is the sacrifice itself and the method is the performance of the various limbs of the sacrifice.

It is evident that Bhaṭṭanāyaka's *bhāvanā* is exactly modelled after the concept of the Mīmāṁsakas. This is evident from the refutation of the views of Bhaṭṭanāyaka by Abhinavagupta, who argues that in the threefold *bhāvanā* mentioned by him, the operational part is nothing but *vyañjanā*.[3] Here Bhaṭṭanāyaka seems to have maintained that poetry itself, through the power of *bhāvanā* existing in it, like the injunctive power existing in Vedic prescriptions, makes the *rasa* enjoyable. Poetic language has the inherent power of *bhāvanā*, by virtue of which the particular incidents described in a poem shed their special and temporal specificity, and becomes capable of universal enjoyment.

Abhinavagupta counters the above by demonstrating that in such a *bhāvanā*, the actual process is that of poetic suggestion, the manner in which a poem converts *rasa* into an enjoyable object is by adhering to propriety in the selection of *guṇa*s and *alaṁkāra*s. In other words, *rasa* conveyed through poetry becomes enjoyable due to the propriety in expression and through the power of suggestion. Hence in his view, Bhaṭṭanāyaka's notion of *bhāvanā* is redundant.

Bhaṭṭanāyaka seems to have used the Mīmāṁsā model of

---

[3] *tasmād vyañjakatvākhyena vyāpāreṇa guṇālaṁkāraucityādikayā itikartavyatayā kāvyam bhāvakam rasān bhāvayati iti tryamśāyām api bhāvanāayām karaṇāṁśe dhvananam eva nipatati*

– Ānandavardhana 1940: 189

sacrifice to explain the process of universalization (*sādhāraṇīkaraṇa*) which is his unique contribution to aesthetics. The following *kārikās* ascribed to him, quoted by Hemacandra in his *Kāvyānuśāsana*, would make the point clear:

> *ārogyam āptavan sāmbaḥ stutvā devam aharpatim* ।
> *syād arthāvagatiḥ pūrvam ityādivacane yathā* ॥
> *tatascopāttakāladinyakkāreṇopajāyate* ।
> *pratipattur manasy evam pratipattir na saṁśayaḥ* ॥
> *yaḥ ko'pi bhāskaram stauti sa sarvo 'pyagado bhavet* ।
> *tasmād aham api staumi roganirmuktaye ravim* ॥
> – Nandi 2007: 215

"Sāmba attained health by extolling the Sun god". On hearing this, first of all there will be the cognition of its meaning. Thereafter, it is doubtless that there will arise this cognition in the mind of the hearer superseding the time and place mentioned. Anybody who extols the Sun god will become healthy. Therefore I am going to extol him for being freed from illness.

Bhaṭṭanāyaka refers to the Mīmāṁsā position that on hearing the statement that Sāmba attained health by praising the Sun god, a person cognizes the universal element in the statement which transcends its time–space frame: anybody praising the Sun god can attain health. The same process happens in poetry, wherein emotions are cognized by the reader in their universal realm, transcending time and space, through the process of universalization (*sādhāraṇīkaraṇa*).

III

Syntax is an interesting area wherein the Mīmāṁsakas have done extensive philosophical explorations. Poeticians like Mahima Bhaṭṭa have found such discussions very useful in tackling stylistic issues in poetic language. For example, the use of negation in the subject phrase of a sentence will yield a totally different meaning in comparison with the same negation used in the predicate. Thus the difference between "the brāhmaṇa is not coming" and "the nonbrāhmaṇa is coming" is huge. As per the Mīmāṁsā terminology, the former is prohibition of the relevant (*prasajyapratiṣedha*) and the latter exclusion (*paryudāsa*). The resultant defect due to such mix-up in such instances is designated *vidheyāvimarśa* by Mahima Bhaṭṭa.

The most significant Mīmāṁsā dictum accepted by Mahima Bhaṭṭa is his view that all verbal statements point to some object to be accomplished (*sarva eva śābdo vyavahāraḥ sādhyasādhanabhāvagarbhatayā prāyeṇanumānarupo 'vagantavyaḥ* – *Vyaktiviveka*, p. 140). This is a well-known position of the Prābhākaras that "all utterance should be relevant to some context in practical life and therefore point to an action as its ultimate meaning" (Hiriyanna 1994: 318). The well-known *Mīmāṁsāsūtra*: *āmnāyasya kriyārthathvād ānarthakyamatadarthānām* (1.2.1) similarly reiterates that the whole of Vedic discourse has some ritualistic act as the ultimate meaning.

However, in his analysis of language, Mahima Bhaṭṭa treads an independent path and maintains that the cognitive process in language is always of the nature of inference – a position which will not be acceptable to Mīmāṁsakas who accept verbal testimony as a *pramāṇa* independent of inference. According to Mahima Bhaṭṭa, meanings of all sentences, if analysed, could be split into the subjective (*anuvādya*) and predicative (*vidheya*) portions. The predicated element is substantiated by the subjective element. Therefore, if a sentence gives a meaning that "*A* is *B*", it has an internal structure as "*A* therefore *B*". For example, the sentence, "The aged king went to the forest" could mean that the king went to the forest *because he was aged*. Another point where Mahima Bhaṭṭa differs from the Mīmāṁsakas is with relation to the acceptability of presumption (*arthāpatti*) as an independent *pramāṇa*. While the Mīmāṁsakas assert its independent nature, Mahima Bhaṭṭa maintains that it can be included in inference.

Another significant point on which Mahima Bhaṭṭa differs from the Prābhākaras is that he does not accept their position that words have inherent power to denote meaning, like an arrow which has the capacity to hit its target, piercing through all the intermediary obstacles at one stretch. The operation of an arrow is purely autonomous, but the operation of the word giving out its meaning is not so. It is based on convention (*saṅketa*). A word cannot generate a meaning if it does not have a conventional meaning assigned to it. If this is not accepted, any meaning could be cognized from any word. Mahima Bhaṭṭa maintains that all the senses cognized from the linguistic expression other than its conventional one are inferred (*anumeya*).

Many other works on poetics also, especially the *Kāvyaprakāśa* of Mammaṭa, contain profuse references to Pūrva-Mīmāṁsā positions on a number of occasions. For example, when Mammaṭa, describing the sense of words, refers to the view *saṅketitaḥ caturbhedo jātyādir jātir eva vā* the second view is that of Jaimini, who as per the *sūtra, ākṛtistukriyārthatvād* (I.3.333) makes *jāti* or the class attribute of the sense of a word. In the passage *phalam samvittiḥ prakaṭatā vā* (Dwivedi 1986: 42). Also, Mammaṭa adapts the Mīmāṁsā view that the result of knowledge is knownness (*jñātatā*). Another area wherein Mīmāṁsā has influenced Sanskrit poetics is that of figures of speech. The figure *arthāpatti*, accepted by poeticians from the time of Viśvanātha and Ruyyaka, is evidently derived from the fifth *pramāṇa* accepted by the Mīmāṁsakas. So is the case with *parisaṁkhyā*, accepted by Rudraṭa, Mammaṭa and Viśvanātha as a figure, which occurs in Jaimini (I.2.34, III.7.33).

From all this, one can conclude that Pūrva-Mīmāṁsā has considerably enriched the thought processes and basic concepts of Alaṁkāraśāstra. Probably, Appaya Dīkṣita's work on poetics, the *Citramīmāṁsā*, is a tribute to this enduring relationship.

10

Influence of Buddhist Philosophy on Mahima Bhaṭṭa

I

MAHIMA Bhaṭṭa, the author of *Vyaktiviveka* was a versatile scholar, erudite in a number of disciplines like Śaivism, Grammar, Mīmāṁsā and Buddhism. A perusal of the *Vyaktiviveka* is enough to vouchsafe this fact, as is evident from the learned discussions contained in the text, on a variety of philosophical and technical problems like the nature of language, syntactical structures, verbal cognition, perception and inference (Rajendran 1991: 44-51). Mahima Bhaṭṭa not only betrays familiarity with philosophical standpoints taken by various systems, but also makes use of technical terms and key concepts evolved in various systems. The influence of the tenets of Kashmiri Śaivism on Mahima Bhaṭṭa has been brought forth by K.C. Pandey (1950: 325-35). However, a study of the *Vyaktiviveka* shows that the medieval logic evolved by the Buddhist philosophers Diṅnāga and Dharmakīrti has also exerted much influence on Mahima Bhaṭṭa's thought. This paper aims to trace out the extent of Buddhist influence on this most remarkable poetician belonging to the antagonist camp of the *dhvani* theory.

II

It is Bhaṭṭagopāla, the commentator of *Kāvyaprakāśa* who for the first time pointed out that Mahima Bhaṭṭa was indeed influenced by Buddhist thought. When discussing the views of Mahima Bhaṭṭa on *vyañjanā* in the Vth *ullāsa* of *Kāvyaprakāśa*, Bhaṭṭagopāla introduces the former as *saugatamatānusārenānum ānaikapradhāno mahimā*.[1] Similarly, Ruyyaka, the commentator of *Vyaktiviveka* seems to assume on several occasions the Buddhist orientation of Mahima Bhaṭṭa's thought. Thus, commenting on Mahima Bhaṭṭa's conclusion of *lakṣaṇā* in *anumāna*, he makes the interesting observation that though Buddhists accept *lakṣaṇā* as an *arthavyāpāra*, it should actually be considered as *anumāna*, thereby suggesting that Mahima Bhaṭṭa subscribed to Buddhist positions in such matters.[2] Again, on Mahima Bhaṭṭa's comment that pain is a specific form of experience, he observes that "this has been stated as per Buddhist principles".[3] Similarly, when Mahima Bhaṭṭa points out that we cognize a particular type of bird characterized by *garuḍatva* from the line *mohaṁ harer vihaṅgamo hantu*, Ruyyaka explains that *garuḍatva* is reckoned as a class characteristic as per Buddhist principles according to which *garuḍa*s are many.[4] From all these, it is obvious that Buddhist philosophy exerted great influence on Mahima Bhaṭṭa, though he was a Śaivite in his basic orientation.

III

The influence of medieval Buddhist logic as developed by Diṅnāga and Dharmakīrti is discernible in a pronounced manner in Mahima Bhaṭṭa's concept of *anumāna*, wherein he includes all varieties of *dhvani*. According to Ānandavardhana, the so-called suggested meaning (*vyaṅgyārtha*) is revealed to a man of taste by a power called *vyañjanā*, which exists in word and sense, in addition to the normal functions of *abhidhā* and *lakṣaṇā*. Mahima Bhaṭṭa disputes

---

[1] *Sāhityacūḍāmaṇi* of Bhaṭṭagopāla and the Commentary on *Kāvyaprakāśa* of Mammaṭa, ed. R. Harihara Sastri, p. 153.

[2] Ruyyaka, *Vyaktiviveka-vyākhyāna*, ed. Rewaprasada Dwivedi, p. 48.

[3] Ibid., p. 376.

[4] Ibid., p. 279.

this claim and establishes that words do not have any power save *abhidhā*, the denotative function and all the other senses are just intelligent deductions from the denoted meaning, made by a discerning reader. He avers that both the secondary meaning (*lakṣyārtha*) and the suggested meaning (*vyaṅgyārtha*) are thus deduced meanings, inferred from the expressed meaning. He also demonstrates that there is invariable concomitance between the expressed meaning and the secondary/suggested meanings.

Mahima Bhaṭṭa's concept of invariabale concomitance is based on the notions of causality (*tadutpatti*) and identity (*tādātmya*). Accordingly, two facts are deemed to be invariably related if one is the cause of the other and if both are identical. Thus smoke and fire are related through causal connection; and since there will always be fire if there is smoke, we can infer the former from the latter. Similarly, *āmra* "mango tree" and "tree" are having the relationship of identity and when we know that a thing is *āmra*, we can infer that it is a tree. This is an instance of the identical relation existing between genus and species. Mahima Bhaṭṭa follows the above Buddhist position in his concept of *anumāna*, wherein he includes all instances of *vyaṅgya-vyañjaka-bhāva*. The following *saṅgrahakārikā*s of *Vyaktiviveka* make his position clear:

> *vācyapratyayayor nāsti vyaṅgyavyañjakatārthayoḥ* ।
> *tayoh pradīpaghaṭavat sāhityenāprakāśanāt* ॥
> *pakṣadharmatva.sambandhavyāptisiddhivyapekṣaṇāt* ।
> *vr̥kṣatvāmratvayor yadvat yadvac cānaladhūmayaḥ* ॥
> *anumānatvam evātra yuktaṁ tallakṣaṇānvayāt* ।
>
> – *Vyaktiviveka* I, pp. 33-35

The main difference between the positions of Buddhists and Naiyāyikas is that the former insists that in invariable concomitance, there should be "an inner necessity connecting the two terms of the relation". While to the latter mere invariable presence is necessary between the major and minor terms. To illustrate, the former will not accept propositions like "all animals with cloven hoofs have horns", which will be perfectly acceptable to the latter (Hiriyanna 1994: 201). This major difference is lost sight of by some historians of poetics who wrongly make Mahima Bhaṭṭa a follower of Nyāya logic.

Mahima Bhaṭṭa makes use of the cause–effect relationship to explain most of the instances of *dhvani* and the relation of identity to explain the *arthāntarasaṅkramitavācya* – sub-variety of *avivakṣitavācya*. We can illustrate his concept of *vyāpti* based on causal relationship in the following example:

> Oh, ascetic, you can wander freely since that dog has been killed by the lion on the banks of Godāvarī.

Here the presence of the lion is the probans; the undesirability of wandering the probandum; and their invariable concomitance is based on direct cause–effect relationship.[5]

Mahima Bhaṭṭa makes use of the relationship of identity to explain the cognition of meaning in instances like the following, which employ proper nouns like "Rāma" in a suggestive manner.

> "I am Rāma, I shall withstand everything".

Here the word *rāma* does not simply give forth the idea of an individual called Rāma. On the other hand, it conveys the idea of the person Rāma, who has endured many calamities and mishaps in his life, all of which are understood by the reader as per the context. The relationship between Rāma the individual and Rāma who is hardened by the endurances of calamities of life is that of identity (*tādātmya*), as between a tree and a *śiṁśapā*.[6]

IV

Another salient feature of Mahima Bhaṭṭa's logic, which shows Buddhist influence, is that it allows the possibility of indirect relations also, based on negation just like direct relation based on the presence of the minor term. Dharmakīrti speaks of eleven of such examples, viz.

1. *svabhāvānupalabdhi* (simple negation contained in all types

---

[5] *Vyaktiviveka*, p. 463.

[6] Ibid., p. 474.

of negative perceptual judgement),

2. *kāryānupalabdhi* (negation of effect, on the basis of which negation of its efficient case is inferred),
3. *vyāpakānupalabdhi* (deduction of the negation of one fact from the negation of another fact),
4. *svabhāvaviruddhopalabdhi* (affirmation of an incompatible fact, from which the negation of its counterpart follows),
5. *viruddhakāryopalabdhi* (affirmation of an incompatible effect from which the negation of the counterpart of its cause follows),
6. *viruddhavyāptopalabdhi* (affirmation of an incompatible subordinate),
7. *kāryaviruddhopalabdhi* (affirmation of incompatibility with the effect),
8. *vyāpakaviruddhopalabdhi* (affirmation of incompatibility with an inconclusive fact),
9. *kāraṇānupalabdhi* (negation of cause),
10. *kāraṇa-viruddhopalabdhi* (affirmation of incompatibility with the cause of the denied fact), and
11. *kāraṇaviruddhakāryopalabdhi* (affirmation of effect, produced by something incompatible with the cause of the denied fact) (Stcherbatsky 1993: 370-81).

Mahima Bhaṭṭa makes use of some of the above formulae in his explanation of the cognition of the suggested meaning. The following instances may be cited:

> Oh mendicant, wander freely, since that dog has been killed by the lion.

According to Mahima Bhaṭṭa, this is an example of either *svabhāvaviruddhopalabdhi* or *vyāpakaviruddhopalabdhi*. In the former case, the cause is the presence of the lion and the effect is free wandering, and since they are mutually incompatible, the presence of the former leads one to the conclusion of the absence of the latter.[7]

In the case of *vyāpakaviruddhopalabdhi*, the inferred meaning – the absence of the act of wandering – is generated by misgivings of danger, the absence of which is the major premise for action.

An instance of *kāraṇānupalabdhi*:

> Himālaya could not give his daughter to Śiva since the latter had not requested for it.

Here the absence of the request is the reason for the absence of the act of giving.[8]

V

There are many other minor points in Mahima Bhaṭṭa's *Vyaktiviveka* which also indicate the extent of the influence of Buddhist philosophy on him. Thus, Dharmakīrti's argument that illustrative example is not a necessary part of syllogism is accepted by Mahima Bhaṭṭa also. Mahima Bhaṭṭa, while substantiating the argument that all linguistic statements are propositions, refers to the opponents' view that in that case, all sentences should also contain illustrative examples. He counters this view by citing the arguments of Dharmakīrti himself, who maintains that examples are not necessary for a learned person.

> *tadbhāvahetubhāvau hi dṛṣṭānte tadavedinaḥ khyāpyete viduṣāṁ vācyo hetur eva hi tādṛśaḥ*[9]

> The relationships of identity and causation are made known through illustrative examples only in the case of an ignorant person. In the case of really learned people, the mention of reason will suffice.

Mahima Bhaṭṭa also maintains that in a syllogism, it is not necessary to mention *pratijñā* (thesis) and *nigamana* (conclusion)

---

[7] *Vyaktiviveka*, pp. 463-66.

[8] *Vyaktiviveka*, p. 53.

[9] *Pramāṇavārttika* II, p. 27.

separately, as they are implied. He cites a relevant passage from an anonymous source:

> *pratijñāyāḥ eva tāvad garnyamānārthāyāḥ vacanaṁ punarvacanam kiṁ punar asyāḥ punarvacanam ity apārthakaṁ nigamanam*[10]

Diṅnāga and Dharmakīrti also maintain that "the real members of a syllogism are the general rule and its application, to an individual instance", viz. *avinābhāva* and *pakṣadharmatā* (Stcherbatsky 1993: 280). Evidently, this must be the source of Mahima Bhaṭṭa's position.

Another important philosophical position adopted by Mahima Bhaṭṭa on Buddhism is the difference he maintains between the objects perceived in direct perception and comprehended through language. According to him, objects have got two aspects, viz. the generic and the specific. The former is a mental construct (*vikalpa*) and can be understood only through the use of language. The latter is revealed only through direct perception. However, poets endowed by the gift of imagination are able to visualize this specific aspect and depict it through the figure of *svabhāvokti*.[11]

It seems that Mahima Bhaṭṭa's views are influenced by the distinction made and maintained in Buddhist thought between *svalakṣaṇa*, the "thing-in-itself" directly comprehended in perception and *sāmānya lakṣaṇa*, the generic aspect, the aspect comprehended through inference. In the words of Th. Stcherbatsky:

> The doctrine that there are two and only two sources of knowledge means that there are two radically distinct sources of cognition, the one which is a reflex of ultimate reality and the other which is a capacity of constructing the images in which this reality appears in the phenomenal world. ... In perception, the image of the object is cognized directly; i.e. vividly. In inference, it is cognised indirectly, i.e. vaguely, or abstractly through its mark. – 1993: 74

---

[10] *Vyaktiviveka*, p. 443.

[11] Ibid., p. 452.

Mahima Bhaṭṭa maintains that the meaning comprehended through language also is generic, as in inference, but in *svabhāvokti*, this limitation is somehow transcended.

VI

We see decisive influence of Buddhist outlook in Mahima Bhaṭṭa's thought at a deeper metaphysical level also. Mahima Bhaṭṭa maintains that even though the *vibhāva*s, *anubhāva*s and *vyabhicārī-bhāva*s presented through poetry are unreal, they give forth inference of *rasa*, which culminates in moral instructions of the dos and don'ts of life. As to how an illusory knowledge can serve such a practical function, Mahima Bhaṭṭa refers to the following *kārikā* of *Pramāṇavārttika* which reiterates the practical efficacy of even false knowledge

> *maṇipradīpaprabhayor maṇibuddhyābhidhāvatoḥ mithyā-jñanāviśeṣe 'pi viśeṣo'rthakriyām prati*[12]
>
> Between two persons who run towards the lustres of jewel and lamp, mistaking them to be jewel, even though there is agreement in false knowledge, there is difference with regard to practical efficacy.

Thus, the person mistaking the lustre of jewel for jewel itself finally takes hold of it following the leads given by false knowledge. This illustrates the Buddhist position:

> Knowledge may have value for life, but its metaphysical significance is next to nothing. – Hiriyanna 1994: 209

Mahima Bhaṭṭa finds this a handy formula to explain the aesthetic world, which, bereft of objective reality still possesses practical utility. He maintains that it will be ridiculous if we apply the test of validity to the facts presented in fiction and designates inference in the realm of imagination as *kāvyānumiti*, thus bracketing it from ordinary inference, which is a means of valid knowledge.

---

[12] *Pramāṇavārttika* I, p. 57.

VII

Thus, a close study of the *Vyaktiviveka* will bring forth the extent and depth of Buddhist influence on Mahima Bhaṭṭa. Nevertheless, Mahima Bhaṭṭa does not seem to be influenced by the religious side of Buddhism in the least, as he was a staunch follower of Kashmiri Śaivism. He does not seem to be influenced by the Apoha theory of language either, as he believed that words denote positive meanings. In short, Mahima Bhaṭṭa can be taken to be a logician anchored to traditional theology and religion, who nevertheless made profuse use of concepts of medieval Buddhist logic.

11

References to Buddhist Philosophy in Dhvanyāloka

ĀNADNAVARDHANA'S *Dhvanyāloka*,[1] unlike many other treatises on poetics, is a work dealing with several topics related to philosophy. The reason for this is the fact that the establishment of the *dhvani* theory necessitates the discussion of several semantic problems which had been discussed by grammarians and exponents of different systems of philosophy like Mīmāṁsā and Nyāya. Another great branch of philosophy which has made significant contribution to semantics, especially its philosophical and logical aspects is Buddhism. A relatively unexplored field in the study of *Dhvanyāloka* is its references to Buddhist philosophy. Ānandavardhana, it is true, refers to Buddhism only on a limited number of occasions in the *Dhvanyāloka*. However, these references themselves are very fascinating.[2]

Ānandavardhana's Commentary on a Buddhist Work

It is very interesting to note that Ānandavardhana has, as per his own words, contributed one work to the Buddhist literature. While dealing with the view that *dhvani* is inexplicable, he maintains that he has examined the doctrine of inexplicability, professed by

---

[1] यत् तु अनिर्देश्यत्वं सर्वलक्षणविषयं बौद्धानां प्रसिद्धम्, तत् तन्मतपरीक्षायां ग्रन्थान्तरे निरूपयिष्यामः। – 1940: 519

[2] Abhinavagupta, *Locana*, p. 519

ग्रन्थान्तर इति। विनिश्चयटीकायां धर्मौतर्यां या विवृतिरमुना ग्रन्थकुता कृता तत्रैव तद्व्याख्यातम्।

Buddhists, in a separate work.

Here, Abhinavagupta makes the clarification that the work written by Ānandavardhana is the *Vivṛti* on the *Pramāṇaviniścayaṭīkā* written by Dharmottara (Masson and Patwardhan 1985: 192). It is indeed surprising that professed Hindu author as he is, Ānandavardhana should have ventured to write a commentary on a Buddhist work. Masson and Patwardhana point out:

> To our knowledge, there is no commentary by a Hindu writer on a Buddhist text. The work, therefore, would be unique.[3]

Though the nature of Ānandavardhana's *Pramāṇaviniścaya-ṭīkāvivṛti* cannot be determined, it seems that it was a work refuting Buddhist principles. It is in the context of criticizing the doctrine of inexplicability that Ānandavardhana refers to the work. Further Ānandavardhana's philosophical affiliation to Vaiṣṇavism, evidenced by the *maṅgala-śloka* of *Dhvanyāloka* and another verse cited in it seem to exclude any possibility of his relationship with Buddhism. The custom of writing critical commentaries is not strange in India, either. Ruyyaka's commentary on Mahima Bhaṭṭa's *Vyaktiviveka* and Nāgeśa Bhaṭṭa's commentary on Jagannātha Paṇḍit's *Rasagaṅgādhara* are critical as well as explanatory. Hence there is nothing wrong in assuming that Ānandavardhana's *Vivṛti* on *Pramāṇaviniścaya-ṭīkā* was also a critical exposition.

Dharmottara, the author of *Pramāṇaviniścaya-ṭīkā*, was a prolific writer on Buddhist logic. According to Satischandra Vidyabhusana (1988: 329), he belonged to about 847 CE.

The following works are assigned to him:

i. *Nyāyabindu-ṭīkā*: A commentary on Dharmakīrti's *Nyāyabindu*.

ii. *Pramāṇaparīkṣā*: Which is lost and which exists only in a

---

[3] Ānandavardhana, 1940: 508-09:

या व्यापारवती रसान् रसयितु काचित्कवीनां नवा
दृष्टिर्या परिनिष्ठतार्थविषयोन्मेषा च वैपश्चिती।

ते द्वे अप्यवलम्ब्य विम्मनिशं निर्वर्णयन्तो वयं
श्रान्ता नैव च लब्धमब्धिशयन! त्वद्-भक्तितुल्यं सुखम्।।

Tibetan translation.

iii. *Apohanāma-prakaraṇa*: Existing only in a Tibetan translation. The Sanskrit original is lost.

iv. *Kṣaṇapabhaṅga-siddhi*: Existing only in a Tibetan translation.

v. *Paraloka-siddhi*: Existing only in a Tibetan translation.

vi. *Pramāṇaviniścaya-ṭīkā*: This is also lost. Existing only in a Tibetan translation (Vidyabhusana, 1988: 329-31).

The last work, on which Ānandavardhana wrote his *Vivṛti* is a commentary on the *Pramāṇaviniścaya* of Dharmakīrti, a work lost and available only in a Tibetan translation. Vidyabhusana records that the work has three chapters: (1) System of Perception, (2) Inference for One's Own Self, and (3) Inference for the Sake of Others (ibid.: 309). From this, is clear that the topics discussed by Ānandavardhana in his *Vivṛti* were related to Buddhist epistemology.

The Doctrine of Anirvacanīyatva

While dealing with the problem whether *dhvani* is beyond the scope of words (*vācām aviṣaye sthita*), Ānandavardhana poses the *pūrva-pakṣa* from a purely empirical standpoint and also as a metaphysical question (Ānandavardhana 1940: 163). To the empirical objection, the answer is simple: *dhvani* is not undefinable since its nature can be described clearly. If, in spite of the general and special definitions given to *dhvani*, its indefinability is insisted upon, any object could be described as undefinable (ibid.: 162ff., 517ff.).

It is in connection with the metaphysical *pūrva-pakṣa* that Ānandavardhana refers to the Buddhist doctrine of *anākhyeyatva*. According to this doctrine, everything in the world is inexplicable (*anirvacanīya*). Ānandavardhana explicitly refers to the doctrine as that advocated by Buddhists (1940: 163). This *pūrva-pakṣa* is introduced by Abhinavagupta with the citation of some passages:[4]

1. नार्थं शब्दाः स्पृशन्त्यपि
2. अनिर्देश्यस्य वेदकम्

It has not been possible to reconstruct the cited verses here

[4] Abhinavagupta, *Locana*, p. 519.

or to trace their source. However, it seems that the view referred to here is the Buddhist theory of Apoha. Kunjunni Raja (1977: 78) points out that according to the Buddhists:

> Words deal directly with conceptual images which are purely subjective constructions of the mind (*vikalpas*) and therefore, there can be no real connection between words and the external object.

It can be seen that the passages *nārthaṁ, śabdāḥ* and *spr̥śintyapi* deal with the same problem and deny the connection between words and objects.

Ānandavardhana meets this objection by citing the analogy of the Buddhist compromise of the doctrine of indefinableness when they define perception. Perception, as per Buddhist tenets, defies any conceptual or linguistic interpretation since the sensory knowledge deals with the unique characteristic of the perceived object without the help of any other knowledge and since the sense data are too unique to be translated into language. Thus, strictly speaking, perception like any reality is indefinable. Still there is a definition for perception in Buddhism. Similarly, Ānandavardhana contends, *dhvani* may be indefinable theoretically; still we can have a definition of *dhvani*.[5] In other words, the definition of *dhvani* can be accommodated even in the framework of Buddhist doctrine of indefinableness.

Ānandavardhana's Reference to Dharmakīrti

It is interesting to note that *Dhvanyāloka* contains references to the great Buddhist logician, Dharmakīrti. Ānandavardhana traces the authorship of an anonymous verse to Dharmakīrti, when discussing the implications of that verse. The verse is as follows:[6]

लावण्यद्रविणव्ययो न गणित: क्लेशो महान् स्वीकृत:
स्वच्छन्दस्य सुखं जनस्य वसतश्चिन्तानलो दीपित:।

---

[5] Aandavardhana, 1940: 519:
बौद्धमतेन या तथा प्रत्यक्षादिलक्षणं तथाऽस्माकं ध्वनिलक्षणं भविष्यति।

[6] Cited in the *Vr̥ti* of the 3rd Udyota of *Dhvanyāloka*.

एषाऽपि स्वयमेव तुल्यरमणाभावाद्वराकी हता
कोऽर्थश्चेतसि वेधसा विनिहितन्व्यास्तनुं तन्वता।।

*lāvaṣyadraviṇavyayo na gaṇitaḥ kleśo mahān svīkṛtaḥ
svacchandasya sukhaṁ janasya vasataścintānalo dīpitaḥ* ।

*eṣā 'pi svayameva tulyaramaṇābhāvādvarākī hatā
ko 'rthaścetasi vedhasā vinihitanvyāstanuṁ tanvatā* ।।

Here Ānandavardhana discusses the problem whether the *alaṁkāra* is Vyājastuti, a veiled eulogy of the heroine through the expressed condemnation. This involves some difficulty with regard to the speaker. We cannot assume that the speaker is a lover, since the lover will not say that the heroine is frustrated for want of a suitable lover. Nor can the speaker be a detached person, since such a person will not indulge in musings of this nature. Ānandavardhana maintains that, dealing as it is with the pain, of the obscurity of a genius, the verse is a case of *aprastutapraśaṁsā*. Tracing the verse to Dharmakīrti, he shows that it is actually the lamentation of the author over the sad plight of his philosophy which stands frustrated on account of the fact that there is no suitable recepient for it. In order to show that this particular thought is frequently seen in Dharmakīrti, Ānandavardhana cites the following verse from the former's *Pramāṇavārttika*:[7]

अनध्यवसितावगाहमनल्पधी शक्तिना
प्यदृष्टपरमार्थतत्वमधिकाभियोगैरपि।

मतं मम जगत्यलब्धसहशप्रतिग्राहकं
प्रयास्यति पयोनिधेः पय इव स्वदेहे जराम्।।

*anadhyavasitāvagāhamanalpadhī śaktinā
pyadṛṣṭaparamārthatatvamadhikābhiyogairapi* ।

*mataṁ mama jagatyalabdhasahaśapratigrāhakaṁ
prayāsyati payonidheḥ paya iva svadehe jarām* ।।

Ānandavardhana and the Buddhist Concept of Svalakṣaṇa

It is clear that Ānandavardhana was also familiar with the

---

[7] Identified by Sternbach 1974: 208.

terminology of Buddhist philosophy. In the fourth *udyota*, where he discusses the problem of how novelty is achieved in poetry, Ānandavardhana observes that the objects of the world differ from each other on the basis of *avasthā*, *deśa*, *kāla* and *svalakṣaṇa*. It can be seen that *svalakṣaṇa* is a Buddhist concept. It refers to the unique particular that every individual object is.[8] Like the Buddhists, Ānandavardhana subscribes to the view that all objects in the universe are mutually different on account of their unique self-chartacter.[9]

From such stray references to Buddhist philosophy in the *Dhvanyāloka*, it can be seen that Ānandavardhana was well-versed in many concepts of Buddhism. However, while he devotes considerable space for examining and refuting the arguments that classical systems of philosophy like Nyāya and Mīmāṁsā would raise against the *dhvani* theory, Ānandavardhana refers to Buddhist arguments only in a cursory manner. The reason for this seems to be the fact that during the times of Ānandavardhana, Buddhist logic and philosophy must have been relegated to the background by the advent of epistemology in the orthodox systems of philosophy as well as in grammar.

---

[8] For a comparison between *svalakṣaṇa* and the "thing in itself" of Kant, see Hiriyanna, 1994: 201.

[9] Ānandavardhana, 1940: 538.

12

Influence of Nyāya–Vāiśeṣika Philosophy on Alaṁkāraśāstra

IT GOES without saying that all types of scientific discourses, whether old or new, require a vigorous methodology for conceptualization and presentation of their precepts and principles. Logic is the firm foundation on which our methodological principles rest. Hence, logic has been acclaimed as an indispensable tool in all classical traditions, Eastern and Western. In India, the logical system variously designated as Ānvīkṣikī, Nyāya–Vaiśeṣika and Tarka, at different points of time, has been always recognized as an absolute must in education. Kauṭilya elevates Ānvīkṣikī to the status of a lamp lighting up all Śāstras; the saying *kaṇādam pāṇinīyam ca sarvaśāstropakārakam* brings forth the importance of Nyāya–Vaiśeṣika on all types of scientific discourses.

The Nyāya–Vaiśeṣika system has undergone remarkable transformations several times in the course of its development. In the earlier phase, Vaiśeṣika's orientation was ontological and it tried to map the entire universe through its *padārtha* categorization. Side by side, the Nyāya philosophy also emerged, more as an instrument of argumentation than as an independent school of philosophy. Later, with the advent of Gaṅgeśopādhyāya and his *Nyāyatattvacintāmaṇi*, there was a sea-change in the methodology of the Nyāya thought; epistemological issues came to the foreground and philosophy itself became armed with a sophisticated language with *avacchedaka*s and *avacchinna*s to express sophisticated shades of thought in an accurate manner; yet a third phase in the history of Nyāya–Vaiśeṣika thought witnessed the convergence of both the systems into a Tarkaśāstra.

All these strains of thought have had their impact on Alaṁkāraśāstra.

II

We find that it is Bhāmaha who made use of the insights of the early Nyāya–Vaiśeṣika thought in poetics. Bhāmaha prefaces his discussions with the observation that even Śāstric knowledge, intermingled with the *rasa* of poetry, becomes palatable. People consume even bitter medicine after taking honey. Bhāmaha maintains that *śāstra* topics have a direct bearing on *śāstra-kāvyas*; on the other hand, in poetry proper, they have only an indirect relevance. The fifth *pariccheda* of Bhāmaha's *Kāvyālaṁkāra* is an attempt to use Nyāya–Vāiśeṣika terminology to the poetic discourse in an extensive manner. Bhāmaha refers to eleven types of *doṣas* and illustrates ten of them in the fourth *pariccheda* of *Kāvyālaṁkāra*. The eleventh *doṣa*, arising from the faulty employment of *pratijñā, hetu* and *dṛṣṭānta*, is mainly based on Nyāya–Vaiśeṣika and Bhāmaha devotes the entire fifth *pariccheda* for their consideration. He deals with the definition of concepts like *pramāṇas, pratijñā, hetu, dṛṣṭānta* and their varieties mostly from the standpoint of early Nyāya–Vaiśeṣika and often criticizing the Buddhist positions.

According to Bhāmaha, the Buddhist stand that perception is entirely devoid of mental constructs (*kalpanāpoḍham*) is untenable as predication is necessary for any type of knowledge (*vṛtti*) and the cognition of individuality. He says:

pratyakṣam kalpanāpoḍham sato 'rthāditi kecana
kalpanām namajātyādiyojanām pratijānate ।
samāropaḥ kilaitāvān sadarthālambanam ca tad
jātyādyapohe vṛttiḥ kva kva viśeṣaḥ kutaśca saḥ ॥
– *Kāvyālaṁkāra* V.6-7

Bhāmaha maintains that the theoretical framework of inference accepted in logic is applicable to the poetic discourse also.

Accordingly, defective reasoning caused by defects in the components of inferential cognition is applicable to the thought content expressed in poetry also. Bhāmaha refers to various types of defective reasoning in logic proper and proceeds to show how they manifest in poetry, of course, with some difference.

In a Nyāya syllogism, the first member is called *pratijñā* (a premise) and Bhāmaha defines it as the statement of a subject (*pakṣa*) as qualified with the property which is a matter of dispute (*vivādāspadadharmeṇa dharmī kṛtaviśeṣaṇaḥ | pakṣaḥ tasya ca nirdeśaḥ pratijñetyabhidhīyate* – *Kāvyālaṁkāra* V.12). He refers to the following defects of the *pratijñā*:

Defect	*Definition*	*Example*
Tadarthavirodhinī	Self-contradiction	I am the son of a *yati*
Hetuvirodhinī	Defective cause	There is soul/*prakṛti*
Siddhāntavirodhinī	Contrariness to one's premise	Sound is eternal/non-eternal
Sarvāgamavirodhinī	Contrariness to all Śāstras	Body is pure, *pramāṇa*s are three/non-existent
Prasiddhadharma	Too well-known property	Sound is grasped through the ear
Pratyakṣabādhinī	Contrary to perception	Fire is cold

Bhāmaha further refers to the defects called *hetvābhāsa*s also and maintains that similar defects occur only in Śāstras. In poetry proper, the defects related to logic are slightly different, but similar in structure. Here, *pratijña* seems to signify an oath or a stand taken by an individual and *pratijñā-hāni* its violation. There are four types of this defect, arising out of the violation of *dharma*, *artha*, *kāma* and *kopa*. When Duryodhana, after taking an oath to end his life through *prāyopaveśa*, finally coveted royalty, his action furnishes an example of, *dharma-virodha*. When Yudhiṣṭhira decides to play dice with Śakuni, making the declaration that "I will not decline if invited", this furnishes an instance of *arthavirodhinī pratijñā*. Bhīṣma's vow to remain celibate for the sake of his father furnishes a case of *kāmavirodhinī pratijñā*. When Paraśurāma is defeated by Rāma, he has to go back from his vow that he will exterminate all kṣatriyas and this is an instance of *kopavirodhinī pratijñā*.

Bhāmaha also deals with various types of defects related to *hetu* and *dṛṣṭānta* in *kāvya*. But the text being very corrupt here, it is not always easy to understand the allusions made by him here; nor is it possible for us to be convinced that such defects are very relevant in poetry. Probably, Bhāmaha means that poetry has a thematic content where logical structure is very important and violation of it is always a grave defect – a position later elaborated by Mahima Bhaṭṭa.

III

Mahima Bhaṭṭa has made use of medieval logic in his devastating criticism of the *dhvani* theory which he includes in *anumāna*. This is the theoretical position of later Naiyāyikas also. But as I have shown elsewhere that he seems to be more influenced by Buddhist logic developed by Dharmakīrti rather than by classical Nyāya.[1] Nevertheless, despite the thin line of *sāhacarya-niyama* separating Nyāya concept of logic from that of the Bauddhas which is based on *tādātmya* and *tadutpatti*, for all practical purposes, there seems to be no major difference in their perspectives on logic. Mahima Bhaṭṭa looks upon language as a stimulant triggering of a chain of reasoning in the mind of the reader. According to Mahima Bhaṭṭa, all the meanings other than the expressed meaning are cognized from language through the process of inference. The expressed meaning here acts as the probans and the cognized meaning is the probandum. Their relationship is called *sādhya-sādhana-bhāva*. All this shows the orientation of *mahiman* to medieval logic, particularly that developed by Dharmakīrti, and some of these principles are seen adopted in later Nyāya–Vaiśeṣika.

---

[1] See my paper, "Influence of Buddhist Philosophy on Mahima Bhaṭṭa", *Oriental Journal Tirupati*, 41(1-2): 55-65, 1998. See here Chap. 11.

IV

Now we come to the most significant phase of the influence of Nyāya philosophy on Alaṁkāraśāstra. After the advent of Navya-Nyāya, almost all the systems of philosophy began using its terminology, irrespective of their philosophical predilection. In poetics, it was Jagannātha Paṇḍit who performed this mammoth task. Jagannātha was not a Nyāya philosopher at all; his obvious sympathy was with the Vedānta philosophy. But this did not stand in the way of his rewriting the entire Alaṁkāraśāstra using Navya-Nyāya terminology. The results were remarkable: Alaṁkāraśāstra became more precise and unambiguous; it became a *śāstra* proper. It is remarkable that through the treatment of Jagannātha Paṇḍit, even the theories of earlier thinkers become crystal clear. This will be clear to us if we go through his treatment of various theories on *Rasaniṣpatti*. What was only a rough outline in earlier works like the *Kāvyaprakāśa* or even the *Abhinavabhāratī* now assumed clarity and exhaustiveness. As the entire *Rasagaṅgādhara* is a testimony of the terminological influence of Navya-Nyāya, it is not possible to describe the extent to which Jagannātha is influenced by the philosophy in a small paper like this. Instead, we can take the definition of *kāvya* given by Jagannātha as a case in point. At the very outset, Jagannātha echoes the Nyāya concept of the function of a definition: According to him, a definition of *kāvya* should fulfil the following requirements:

1. It should be the delimiting adjunct of the qualifiedness of poetry (*viśeṣyatāvacchedaka*).
2. It should be able to delimit poetry from non-poetry (*taditarabhedabuddhau śādhakam*).

Accordingly, Jagannātha defines poetry as *ramaṇīyātārthaprati-pādakaḥ-śabdaḥ* and demonstrates how the definition is free from defects like *ativyāpti* and *avyāpti* as in the *Nyāyaśāstra*. He gives more precise definition for each component of the definitions and suggests suitable modifications also. His discussions can be paraphrased as follows:

> Poetry is a word which describes beautiful meaning. "Beautiful" means being the subject of a type of knowledge which generates

> non-worldly pleasure. Non-worldliness is a class attribute belonging to pleasure, also called *camatkāra*, where experience is the only proof. The cause of this pleasure is a type of reflection (*bhāvanā*) characterized by repetition. The qualification is to ward off sentences like "A son is born to you" and "I shall give you money" etc. from the purview of poetry. The pleasure given forth by the knowledge arising from the cognition of such sentences is of the worldly type and hence the definition of poetry does not overlap there.

Finally, Jagannātha gives three modified definitions for poetry, removing all possible defects:

1. The state of being the word, which describes meaning which is the subject of contemplation giving forth aesthetic pleasure.
2. The state of being that, the meaning described by which is the subject of contemplation whose delimiting adjunct is identical with the generator of aesthetic pleasure.
3. The state of being the possessor of the aesthetic pleasure through the relation of the describer of the meaning delimited by its capacity of being the generator of the former.

The first definition is discarded because in collective mode of knowledge (*samūthālambana-jñāna*), there is always the possibility of poetry being mixed up with some other linguistic discourses and since such collective knowledge will generate aesthetic pleasure, the mixed-up non-poetry will also have claims of poetry. On the other hand, in the second definition, "poetryness" (*kāvyatva*) is strictly limited to the actual word whose meaning generates aesthetic pleasure. But this definition, being too wordy, is given up for the final one which combines precision and brevity.

Jagannātha displays his logical acumen and profound scholarship in Nyāya on innumerable occasions of his treatment, especially when it comes to the criticism of rival theorists like Appaya Dīkṣita. Some such instances include his criticism of earlier definitions of poetry, the causes of poetry, various divisions of poetry, functions of language like *abhidhā* and the treatment of individual *alaṁkāras*. His treatment of *upamā* is a classical example of his erudition. Starting with an elegant and simple definition of *upamā* as *sādṛśyam sundaram vākyārthopskārakam upamā*, he demolishes the definitions of the figure given by earlier stalwarts like Mammaṭa, Vidyānātha and Appaya Dīkṣita. However, the entire range of his scholarship is devoted for his profound *śābdabodha-vicāra* in *upamā*. He describes, systematically, the verbal cognition in expressions like the following using profuse Nyāya terminology:

1. *aravindasundaram-mukham: aravinda-nirūpitasādṛśyayo-prayojaka saundaryavad – abhinnam mukham.*
2. *aravindamiva sundaram: aravinda – sadṛśya – prayojaka–aundaryavad-abhinnam mukham.*
3. *aravindamiva: aravinda-nirūpita-sadṛśyavad.*
4. *aravindamiva bhāti: aravinda-sādṛśya-prayojaka-dhīviśeṣyaka.*

V

Another area in Alaṁkāraśāstra which has been influenced by Nyāya–Vaiśeṣika philosophy is the arena of individual *alaṁkāra*s. The logical structure of several *alaṁkāra*s is based on Nyāyaśāstra, especially its categories like cause and effect. The following *alaṁkāra*s can be cited as examples:

1. *Vibhāvanā:* Here the effect comes into existence without cause.
2. *Viśeṣokti*: Here effect does not come into existence even though there is sufficient cause.
3. *Akramātiśayokti*: The simultaneity of cause and effect.
4. *Capalātiśayokti*: The production of the effect at the very mention of the cause.
5. *Atyantātiśayokti*: The reversal of cause and effect.

Many other figures like *kāvyaliṅga*, *arthāntaranyāsa* and *anumāna* make use of similar logical principles.

To sum up, it can be seen that Nyāya–Vaiśeṣika, despite its supposed aridness and dreary nature, has exerted significant influence on Alaṁkāraśāstra.

Bibliography

Abhinavagupta, 1975, *Abhinavabhāratī* on Bharata's *Nāṭyaśāstra*, Baroda: Oriental Institute.

Ānandavardhana, 1940, *Dhvanyāloka*, ed. with *Locana* and *Bālapriyā* commentaries by Pattabhirama Sastri, Varanasi: Choukhamba Sanskrit Series Office.

Arthaśāstra of Kauṭilya, ed. R. Sharma Sastri, Mysore, 1919.

Bhāmaha, 1970, *Kāvyālaṁkāra*, ed. P.V. Naganatha Sastri, 2nd edn, Delhi: Motilal Banarsidass.

Bhāskara, 1915, *Vedāntaśāstrabhāṣya*, Benares: Chowkhambha Sanskrit Series.

Bhattacharyya, Sibajiban (ed.), 2009, *Bhartṛhari and Wittgenstein: Word and Sentence*, New Delhi: Sahitya Akademi.

Brahmasūtrabhāṣya, English tr. Swami Gambhirananda, Kolkata: Advaita Ashrama, 2000.

Brahmasūtrabhāṣya of Śrī Śaṅkarācārya, English tr. Swami Gambhirananda, Advaita Ashrama, Calcutta, 1977.

Chakrabarti, Arindam and Ralph Weber (eds), 2015, *Comparative Philosophy without Borders*, London: Bloomsbury.

Complete Works of Srī Śaṅkarācārya (5 vols), Kalady: Sri Sankaracharya University of Sanskrit, 2012.

Coward, Harold, 1990, *Derrida and Indian Philosophy*, Albany, NJ: SUNY Press.

Dasgupta, Surendranath, 1973, *A History of Indian Philosophy*, vol. I, Delhi: Motilal Banarsidass.

Deshpande, G.T., 1989, *Abhinavagupta*, New Delhi: Sahitya Akademi.

Dwivedi, R.C. (ed.), 1986, *The Poetic Light: Kāvyaprakāśa of Mammaṭa*, Delhi: Motilal Banarsidass.

——— (ed.), 1994, *Studies in Mīmāṁsā*, Delhi: Motilal Banarsidass.

Gnoli, R., 1956, *The Aesthetic Experience according to Abhinavagupta*, Varanasi: Chowkhamba Sanskrit Series Office.

Hiriyanna, M., 1994, *Outlines of Indian Philosophy*, reprint, Delhi: Motilal Banarsidass.

Iyer, S., Venkitasubramoniya, 1976, *Kerala Sanskrit Literature: A Bibliography*, Trivandrum: University of Kerala.

Kelkar, Ashok K., 2002, "What Has Bhartrhari Got to Say on Language?", in *Bhartṛhari and Wittgenstein*, ed. Sibajiban Bhattacharyya, New Delhi: Sahitya Akademi.

Kārikāvalī of Viśvanātha Pañcānana with Muktāvalī, Dinakarī and *Rāmarudrī*, ed. with footnotes by Anantasastri, Bombay: Nirnayasagar Press, 1916.

Krishna, Daya, 1996, *Indian Philosophy: A Counter Perspective*, Delhi: Oxford University Press.

Kunjunni Raja, K., 1963/1977, *Indian Theories of Meaning*, Madras: Adyar Library.

———, 1980, *Contribution of Kerala to Sanskrit Literature*, Madras: University of Madras.

———, 1982, "The Date of Śaṅkara", *Rajasudha*, University of Madras.

Mammaṭa, *Kāvyaprakāśa with Sampradāyaprakāśinī of Śrīvidyācakravartin, and Sāhityacūḍāmaṇi of Bhaṭṭagopāla*, ed. R. Harihara Sastri, Trivandrun Sanskrit Series No. LXXXVIII, 1926.

Manusmṛti, ed. Krishnakumar Koramangalam, Calicut: Drona Publications, 2006.

Manusmṛti, with the Commentary *Mānavārthamuktāvalī* of Kulluka, Bombay: Nirnayasagar Press, 1946.

Masson J.L. and M.V. Patwardhan, 1985, *Śāntarasa and Abhinavagupta's Philosophy of Aesthetics*, Pune: Bhandarkar Oriental Research Institute.

Mehandale, K.C. (ed.), 1991, *Tarkasangraha*, text with *Dipika* Sanskrit Commentary, English tr., a Critical Introduction, Explanatory Notes and Appendices, Delhi: Bharatiya Book Corporation.

Nampoothiri, E. Easwaran, 1996, *Vedāntapaddhati*, Trivandrum: Kerasamskritam Publications.

Nandi, Tapasvi (ed.), 2007, *Kāvyānuśāsana of Hemacandra*, Patan: Hemachandracharya North Gujarat University.

Nārāyaṇa Bhaṭṭa, Melputtur, 1933, *Mānameyodaya*, ed. with English Notes by C. Kunhan Raja and S.S. Suryanarayana Sastri, Adyar, Madras: Theosophical Publishing House.

Nussbaum, Martha, 1997, *Cultivating Humanity: A Classical Defense of Reform in Liberal Education*, Cambridge, MA: Harvard University Press.

Nyāyadarśana: The Sutras of Gotama and the Bhasya of Vatsyayana, Delhi: Chowkhamba Sanskrit Pratishthan, 1978.

Pandey, K.C., 1950, *Indian Aesthetics*, vol. I, pp. 325-35, Banaras: Chowkhamba Sanskrit Series Office.

Pandita, Jagannatha, 1988, *Rasagaṅgādhara*, with the commentaries of Nageśabhaṭṭa and Mathura Nath Sastri, Delhi: Motilal Banarsidass.

Rajarajavarma, Vatakkamkur, 1997, *Keralīyasamskṛtasāhityacaritram*, Kalady: Sri Sankaracharya University of Sanskrit.

Rajendran, C., 1991, *A Study of Mahima Bhaṭṭa's Vyaktiviveka*, Calicut: self published.

Raju, P.T., 1970, *Lectures on Comparative Philosophy*, Pune: University of Poona.

Ramachandradu, P., 1983, *The Contribution of Paṇḍitarāja Jagannātha to Sanskrit Poetics*, Delhi: Nirajana.

Rasagangādhara, Jagannātha Paṇḍit, ed. Mathura Natha Sastri, Delhi: Motilal Banarsidass, 1988.

Saratchandran, K., 1997, "The Influence of Sankara on the Literary and Cultural Heritage of Kerala", in *Śaṅkarācārya*, ed. V. Venkatachalam, New Delhi: Sahitya Akademi.

Sarma, E.R. Srikrishna, 1999, *Vedic Tradition of Kerala*, Calicut: Department of Sanskrit, University of Calicut.

Sarvadarśanasaṁgraha of Mādhava, Bombay, Nirnayasagar Press, 1846.

Sastri, S. Kuppuswami, 1932, *A Primer of Indian Logic*, Madras: The Kuppuswami Sastri Research Institute.

Shah K.J., 2002, "Word and Sentence: Two Perspectives — Bhartṛhari and Wittgenstein", in Bhartṛhari and Wittgenstein, ed. Sibajiban

Bhattacharyya, New Delhi: Sahitya Akademi.

Siddhāntamuktāvalī (Kārikāvalī) of Viśvanātha Pañcānana (2 vols), ed. Paṇḍitarāja Srinarayana Sukla, Varanasi: Chowkhamba Sanskrit Series Office, 2001.

Sternbach, Ludwik, *Mahāsubhāṣita-Saṁgraha*, vol. 1, Hoshiarpur: Vishveshvaranand Vedic Research Institute.

Stcherbatsky, Th., 1993, *Buddhistic Logic*, Delhi: Motilal Banarsidass.

Sundaram, P.K., 1981, *Advaita and Other Systems*, Madras: University of Madras.

Sūtasaṁhitā (3 vols), Anandasrama Sanskrit Series, Poona: Anandasrama, 1924.

The Tattvacintāmaṇi of Gaṅgeśopādhyāya vol I, ed. Pandit Kamakhya Natha Tarkavagisa, Delhi: Motilal Banarsidass, 1974.

Tripathi, Radhavallabh, 2014, *Dharmakīrti*, New Delhi: Sahitya Akademi.

Unni, N.P. (ed.), 1997, *Kokilasandeśa*, Trivandrum: Kerala Samskrtam Publications.

Vāmana Kāvyālaṁkārasūtravṛtti with *Kāmadhenu* Sanskrit Commentary and *Vidyādhari* Hindi Commentary, Varanasi: Chowkhamba Amarabharati Prakashan, 1977.

Veezhinathan, N., 2012, *Complete Works of Śrī Śaṅkarācārya*, Introduction, Kalady: S.S. University of Sanskrit.

Venkitachalam, V. (ed.), 2003, *Sankaracarya*, New Delhi: Sahitya Akademi.

Vidyabhusana, S.C., 1988, *A History of Indian Logic*, Delhi: Motilal Banarsidass.

Vyaktiviveka of Mahima Bhaṭṭa, with *Vyaktiviveka-vyākhyāna* of Ruyyaka, ed. Rewa Prasada Dwivedi, Varanasi: Chowkhamba Sanskrit Sansthan, 1982.

Vyaktiviveka-vyākhyāna, R.P. Dwivedi's edition, Varanasi: Chowkhamba Sanskrit Series Office, 1982.

Wong, David, 1989, "Three Kinds of Incommensurability", in *Relativism: Interpretation and Confrontation*, ed. Michael Krausz, Notre Dame: Notre Dame University Press.

Yājñavalkyasmṛti, with commentary by Aparārka (Anandasrama Sanskrit Granthavali, 46), Pune: Anandasrama, 1903.

Index